For a better quality of life

CAVALIER KING CHARLES
Spaniel

AN OWNER'S GUIDE

Nick Mays

Nick Mays is a long-time dog lover and has kept many breeds over the years, including the Cavalier King Charles Spaniel. He is a journalist who has worked for many publications and was Chief Reporter of *Our Dogs* newspaper for 12 years. He has also written and edited several books on animal care. Nick lives with his partner, children and a small menagerie – including dogs, of course – in Yorkshire, England.

David Taylor B.V.M.S., F.R.C.V.S., F.Z.S.

David Taylor is a veterinary surgeon and author who has worked with a wide spectrum of animal species for many years. Founder of the International Zoo Veterinary Group, he has had patients ranging from the King of Spain's Giant Pandas to gorillas in West Africa and killer whales with frostbite in Iceland. He has written over 100 books on animal matters including many best-selling dog books and seven volumes of autobiography. The latter formed the basis for three series of the BBC television drama *One by One*. He lives in Hertfordshire, England.

Dedication

To Rufus, a Cavalier with a huge personality who lives life to the full... and who doesn't read dog books!

CAVALIER KING CHARLES
Spaniel

AN OWNER'S GUIDE

Nick Mays

**Healthcare by
David Taylor**

First published in 2009 by
Collins, an imprint of
HarperCollins Publishers
77–85 Fulham Palace Road
Hammersmith, London W6 8JB

The Collins website address is:
www.collins.co.uk

Collins is a registered trademark of HarperCollins Publishers Limited
11 10 09
6   5   4   3   2   1

A catalogue record for this book is available from the British Library.

Created by: SP Creative Design
Editor: Heather Thomas
Designer: Rolando Ugolini
Photography: All photography by Rolando Ugolini with the exception of the
following: pages 3, 16, 86, 91, 93, 94 and 95 (Steve Mynott – Honeybet).

ISBN: 978-0-00-727431-4

Printed and bound by Printing Express Ltd., Hong Kong

Acknowledgements
The Breed Standard on pages 18–19 is reproduced by kind permission of
the Kennel Club. The publishers would also like to thank the following
individuals for their help in producing this book: Maryann Hogan (Stavonga
Cavaliers), Steve & Marian Mynott (Honeybet Cavaliers) and Leila Tarabad
(Khatibi Cavaliers). The author would like to thank Elizabeth Evans and
Marianne Brett for their assistance.

Note: Dogs are referred to as 'he' throughout to avoid 'he'/'she' each time or
the rather impersonal 'it'. This reflects no bias towards males, and both sexes
are equally valuable and easy to train.

Contents

PART ONE

YOU AND YOUR DOG

Owning a dog is a huge responsibility but
extremely rewarding. When you decide to welcome
a Cavalier King Charles Spaniel into your home,
you have to consider not only how he will fit into
your lifestyle but also what you can offer him in
return. He will need regular exercise, feeding,
games and companionship as well as daily care.

Chapter 1

History and evolution of the breed

The Cavalier King Charles Spaniel could rightfully be described as the ideal family pet dog. For the family who would like a large dog but have limited space, or who think small is beautiful, the Cavalier is the perfect pet – a big dog in a small, compact body. With his friendly and engaging personality, natural intelligence and a happy-go-lucky nature, this dog proves the point that the best things come in small packages.

The Cavalier occupies a high position in the registration figures for the breed on both sides of the Atlantic and it remains one of the most instantly recognizable of the toy breeds.

Royal patronage

The modern Cavalier King Charles Spaniel is descended from the various types of small toy spaniels that are depicted in so many sixteenth-, seventeenth- and eighteenth-century paintings by great artists, including Gainsborough, Titian, Van Dyck, Stubbs, Reynolds and Romney.

These typically show a small spaniel with a flat head, high-set ears, almond-shaped eyes and a rather pointed nose. It is somewhat longer-limbed than today's more compact Cavalier.

Success under the Stuarts

During Tudor times, toy spaniels were popular as ladies' pets for they were ideally suited to the role of lapdogs

The Cavalier is a big dog in a small, compact body. This is a Ruby coloured Cavalier.

Opposite: Cavaliers gained royal patronage as the favourite breed of King Charles II.

(often used as a means of keeping warm on chilly coach journeys or in vast country houses). However, it was under the Stuart dynasty that the royal title of King Charles Spaniels was bestowed upon them. Contemporary accounts record that King Charles II was seldom seen without two or three such dogs at his heels. Indeed, it is arguable whether the Stuarts' fondness for ever-more extravagant wigs was derived from a love of these spaniels, going so far as to emulate their appearance, with the long sides of the wig mimicking the spaniels' ears. Certainly many of the stylized

Cavalier puppies are particularly appealing, and it is easy to see why so many people fall in love with this attractive breed.

paintings of the time show human beings and dogs with certain similarities: the same foreheads, round eyes and, of course, elaborate tonsure. The King's preference for these little spaniels led them to becoming a popular pet as fashion followed suit.

Indeed, so fond was King Charles II of his little dogs that he issued a royal decree that the King Charles Spaniel should be accepted and granted admission in any public place, even in the august confines of the Houses of Parliament where animals were not usually allowed. This decree is still in existence today in the United Kingdom, and it would be interesting were an adventurous Cavalier owner to try it out on a visit to Westminster. A Black and Tan Cavalier named Magjen True Delight of Devonia (also known as Trudy) did gain free entry to Hampton Court in the 1980s, although her owner had to pay the usual admission charge.

The King Charles was known widely as a 'comforte dog' and doctors even wrote prescriptions with this little dog as the remedy. Some owners were reputed to keep the dogs as a means of deterring fleas and thus avoid the plague.

Decline of the breed

As time went by, however, and with the establishment of the Dutch Court of William of Orange, toy spaniels went out of fashion and were replaced in popularity by the Pug. The King Charles Spaniel was subsequently bred with these dogs, resulting in the similar-shaped head of today's English Toy Spaniel

breed. One notable exception to this trend was the strain of red and white King Charles Spaniels that was bred at Blenheim Palace by various Dukes of Marlborough. These dogs were favoured for their sporting prowess as well as their continued charm as lapdogs. Ultimately, they lent their name to the red-and-white patterned Cavalier, which is known today as the Blenheim.

Ideal show dogs

Whilst small spaniels still had their admirers, most dogs were kept during the eighteenth and early nineteenth centuries as working animals. Simple 'pet dog' ownership was a luxury afforded only to the very rich. In major British cities, such as London, Manchester and Liverpool, the main canine attractions were bull and bear baiting with the larger bull breeds of dogs, and infamous rat pits, where terriers would be placed in a ring with live rats and wagers taken on how many rats a dog could dispatch in a given space of time. Dog fighting was also a popular pastime.

However, during the mid-nineteenth century, with many of these cruel 'sports' being outlawed, some dog owners began to turn more to 'showing off' dogs alongside each other rather than pitting them in combat with each other. In fact, many early dog shows were held in the same public houses where 'ratting' used to take place. In this way, the toy spaniel came back into fashion and was sought after as a show dog. These dogs had flat faces, undershot jaws, and domed skulls with long, low-set ears and large, round frontal eyes – typical of the modern King Charles Spaniel.

When the British Kennel Club was founded in 1873, the King Charles Spaniel became one of the first breeds to have formal standards drawn up and to

be recognized as such. Thus the earlier type of dog, as seen in seventeenth-century paintings and favoured by the Merry Monarch, became all but extinct.

The Cavalier challenge

By the early twentieth century, dog showing was well established in the UK, USA and many European countries.

Cavaliers make great pets for people of all ages, no matter what their lifestyle.

The distinctive Ruby Cavalier is probably less popular than the Blenheim.

Shows, such as Crufts in the UK and Westminster in the United States, were viewed as the pinnacle of the dog showing year. In the mid-1920s, an American Spaniel enthusiast named Roswell Eldridge came to England to search for foundation stock for toy spaniels that resembled those in the old paintings, including one by Sir Edwin Landseer of 'The Cavalier's Dogs'. He was dismayed that all he could find were the short-faced King Charles Spaniels, commonly known as 'Charlies'.

Eldridge tried to get both the Kennel Club and the King Charles fraternity interested in re-establishing the old-type King Charles Spaniel – or the 'Cavalier' type after the famous painting – but his overtures were largely ignored.

However, he was not to be dissuaded and succeeded in persuading the Kennel Club to allow him to offer a cash incentive to breeders to re-create the old-type dogs. He advertised in the 1926 Crufts catalogue, offering prizes at Crufts for three years (later extended to five years) and the princely sum of 25 pounds sterling respectively for the best dog and best bitch of the Blenheim variety, as seen in King Charles II's reign. Eldridge wrote in the Crufts catalogue that he was seeking dogs 'as shown in the pictures of King Charles II's time, long face, no stop, flat skull, not inclined to be domed and with the spot in the centre of the skull'. He stipulated that the prizes would be awarded to the dogs that were nearest to the type described.

Very few King Charles breeders took this challenge seriously as they had worked hard for years to breed out long noses and establish shorter snouts in Charlies. In the first year, only two dogs were entered at the show of the type Eldridge was looking for, but this was sufficient to arouse the interest of a dedicated group of exhibitors and breeders. They worked together and at the next Crufts Show in 1927 Mrs Pitt's bitch 'Waif Julia' took the best bitch prize. In 1928, 'Ann's Son', a dog owned by Miss Mostyn Walker, was awarded the prize but, unfortunately, Roswell

Eldridge had died just one month before Crufts and never saw the results of his challenge prizes.

Evolution of the new breed

In the same year a Club, was founded and the breed's name 'Cavalier King Charles Spaniel' was chosen. It was a conscious decision to keep the close association with the name King Charles Spaniel as many breeders had used long-faced 'rejects' from the kennels of the typical short-faced King Charles Spaniel breeders.

Birth of a new club

In 1928, the new Cavalier King Charles Spaniel Club held its first meeting at Crufts, where the original Standard of the breed was agreed, and, with just some minor alterations, it is much the same wording today. Ann's Son was held up as the desired example of the breed and the breeders agreed that the Cavalier should be 'guarded from fashion', and there was to be no coat trimming or extreme variants bred.

Optional tail docking was agreed as part of the Standard, with no more than one-third of the tail to be removed. However, the law changed in the UK in 2007, banning tail docking for all breeds except dogs bred specifically for working. All Cavaliers born after the introduction of the law will be undocked.

Opposite: This handsome Blenheim Cavalier is alert, inquisitive and energetic. Despite its diminutive size, this breed is notable for its confidence and utter fearlessness, even when faced with aggression from other dogs.

Kennel Club recognition

Although the breeders worked hard, the number of Cavaliers grew, and new colour variants were produced, the Kennel Club still withheld formal recognition of the breed. At the end of the agreed five-year period, it decided that the dogs had not been bred in sufficient numbers, nor were of a single, distinct type to merit a separate, new breed registration from the King Charles Spaniel.

The Cavalier breeders were a determined bunch, however, and throughout the 1930s they continued to breed their dogs. They persuaded some dog show societies to stage special classes for them – where no Challenge Certificates were awarded, of course – and they approached the Kennel Club several times to gain breed recognition.

The onset of World War II put pay to many dog-related leisure activities, but, even then, the KC records show that 60 Cavaliers were registered between 1940 and 1945. Finally, in December 1945 the Kennel Club granted the breed separate registration and awarded Challenge Certificates the following year to allow the Cavalier King Charles Spaniel to gain its own Championships.

American recognition

The breeders continued to fight for recognition in the US. Although in 1961 the American Kennel Club recognized Cavalier King Charles Spaniels by placing the breed in the Miscellaneous classes, it was not until 1995 that Cavaliers were granted full recognition as members of the Toy Group.

Public recognition

In 1963, a Cavalier named Champion Amelia of Laguna, owned by Mrs C. Fryer, won the Toy Group at Crufts, thereby placing the breed firmly in the public spotlight. Ten years later, the Cavalier's reputation as a wonderful family dog was firmly cemented when Messrs Hall and Evans' Alansmere Aquarius won Best In Show at Crufts. There was literally an explosion of interest in Cavaliers and the breed registrations rose accordingly as more and more 'Cavvies' were bred and sold as pets and show dogs.

Sadly, the downside of this surge in popularity led to the Cavalier Club establishing its Rescue and Welfare Service to provide a means of caring for the dogs that had been abandoned, poorly treated or needed re-homing for a variety of reasons. Thankfully, the welfare problems bottomed out eventually, although, still being a popular breed, a large number of Cavaliers continue to find themselves, for a variety of reasons, languishing in breed rescue and animal charity rescue centres each year.

Cavaliers continue to be an immensely popular breed of dog, equally loved as show animals and family pets alike. In 2007, they were ranked as the sixth most popular breed registered by the UK Kennel Club.

Opposite: This tricoloured Cavalier has magnificent ears with lots of feathering. Note his alert, intelligent expression.

The Breed Standard

General appearance Active, graceful and well balanced, with gentle expression.

Characteristics Sporting, affectionate, absolutely fearless.

Temperament Gay, friendly, non-aggressive, no tendency towards nervousness.

Head and skull Skull almost flat between ears. Stop shallow. Length from base of stop to tip of nose about 3.8cm (1½in). Nostrils black and well developed without flesh marks, muzzle well tapered. Lips well developed but not pendulous. Face well filled below eyes. Any tendency to snipiness undesirable.

Eyes Large, dark, round but not prominent; spaced well apart.

Ears Long, set high, with plenty of feather.

Mouth Jaws strong, with a perfect, regular and complete scissor bite, i.e. the upper teeth closely overlapping the lower teeth and set square to the jaws.

Neck Moderate length, slightly arched.

Forequarters Chest moderate, shoulders well laid back, straight legs moderately boned.

Body Short-coupled with good spring of rib. Level back.

Hindquarters Legs with moderate bone; well turned stifle - no tendency to cow hock or sickle hocks.

Feet Compact, cushioned and well feathered.

Tail Length of tail in balance with body, well set on, carried happily but never much above the level of the back. Docking previously optional when no more than one-third was to be removed.

Colours

Tricolour

Blenheim

Gait/Movement Free-moving and elegant in action, plenty of drive from behind. Forelegs and hindlegs move parallel when viewed from in front and behind.

Coat Long, silky, free from curl. Slight wave permissible. Plenty of feathering. Totally free from trimming.

Black and Tan: Raven black with tan markings above the eyes, on cheeks, inside ears, on chest and legs and underside of tail. Tan should be bright. White marks undesirable.

Ruby: Whole coloured rich red. White markings undesirable.

Blenheim: Rich chestnut markings well broken up, on pearly white ground. Markings evenly divided on head, leaving room between ears for much valued lozenge mark or spot (a unique characteristic of the breed).

Tricolour: Black and white well spaced, broken up, with tan markings over eyes, cheeks, inside ears, inside legs, and on underside of tail.

Any other colour or combination of colours most undesirable.

Size Weight: 5.4–8kg (12–18lb). A small, well balanced dog well within these weights desirable.

Faults Any departure from the foregoing points should be considered a fault and the seriousness with which the fault should be regarded should be in exact proportion to its degree and its effect upon the health and welfare of the dog.

Note Male animals should have two apparently normal testicles fully descended into the scrotum.

© The Kennel Club

Ruby

Black and tan

The Cavalier King Charles Spaniel

Eyes
Large, dark, round but not prominent; spaced well apart.

Head and skull
Skull almost flat between ears. Stop shallow. Length from base of stop to tip of nose about 3.8cm (1½in).

Mouth
Jaws strong, with a perfect, regular and complete scissor bite.

Ears
Long, set high, with plenty of feather.

Neck
Moderate length, slightly arched.

Forequarters
Chest moderate, shoulders well laid back, straight legs moderately boned.

Feet
Compact, cushioned and well feathered.

Body
Short-coupled with
good spring of rib.
Level back.

Size
Weight: 5.4–8kg
(12–18lb). A small,
well balanced dog
well within these
weights desirable.

Tail
Length of tail in balance
with body, well set on,
carried happily but
never much above the
level of the back.

Gait/movement
Free-moving and
elegant in action,
plenty of drive from
behind. Forelegs and
hindlegs move parallel
when viewed from in
front and behind.

Hindquarters
Legs with
moderate bone;
well turned stifle
- no tendency to
cow hock or
sickle hocks.

Coat
Long. silky, free from curl.
Slight wave permissible.
Plenty of feathering. Totally
free from trimming.

Chapter 2

Your Cavalier puppy

When you decide that the Cavalier is the right dog for you, the next step is to acquire a puppy. It sounds simple, but before you contemplate bringing a puppy into your home, you have to ask yourself some serious questions and be prepared to answer them honestly. You are going to be responsible for the life of a living creature, and you must be mindful of its welfare.

Questions to ask yourself

Before taking the plunge and buying a Cavalier puppy, you need to examine both your lifestyle and priorities and ask yourself the following questions.

How long will it take?

Are you prepared to look after a dog for all of his life, which, in the Cavalier's case, is, on average, eight to eleven years? A dog is a lifelong commitment, not a temporary acquisition which can be returned if things don't work out in the way you imagined.

Do you have time?

Have you got enough time to spend with a dog? Your Cavalier will need lots of attention as well as regular meals, exercise, obedience training, games and grooming, etc.

Do you work?

Is there somebody at home during the day, or for most of it, who can look after a dog? It is never a good idea to leave a dog alone for more than a few hours each day, especially a puppy. Dogs are sociable pack animals and they need companionship. Some people believe that having two dogs will offset this problem, as they will be company for each other. Although this may be true to

The Cavalier puppy is a small bundle of energy and fun.

a certain extent later in life, two puppies will be just as anxious and needful as one. In any event, dogs need human companionship so that they can learn and adapt to family life. If you leave your dog alone for long periods, it may lead to separation anxiety and a dog that destroys furnishings or soils the house. A puppy needs constant attention, so he cannot be left alone for more than a few minutes at a time.

Is it a family decision?

Does everyone in your family want a dog? This may seem a strange question, but a dog will be not just an item in the house like a TV or an armchair – he will become a member of your family and, as such, needs to be wanted by everyone. Even if one family member says they will be responsible for the dog's care, there will be times when that person cannot do so, in which case somebody else must take over. An adult must have ultimate responsibility for the dog's welfare, because children cannot take on full responsibility for it – no matter how much they might beg, plead and cajole that they will. Never fall into the trap of buying a puppy just 'for the children'. A dog is for the whole family and he will be part of the family.

What will it cost?

Can you afford to care for a dog? The actual purchase price of a puppy, however expensive, is actually a minor consideration when you total up the additional and day-to-day costs of caring for a dog, such as food, vaccinations and general veterinary care. There will also be the initial outlay for equipment, including a bed, bedding, collar and lead, toys, feeding bowls, etc. It is also part of being a responsible dog owner to consider pet insurance, which will obviously help offset the cost of unexpected veterinary bills, as well as microchipping and/or tattooing for the purposes of identification.

Can you keep a dog?

Is your home suitable for a dog, and, if it is rented property, are you allowed to keep a dog there? Ideally, if you are considering owning a dog – even a small breed like a Cavalier – you should have a securely fenced back garden, or at least a shared garden or back yard. This will make it easier for your dog to go outside to toilet and get some basic exercise. Many breeders and, especially, rescue societies will not consider homing a dog to a person living in a high-rise flat or who does not have a properly secured garden. Even if you don't have a garden, this should not completely rule you out from dog ownership, but you have to be prepared to take your dog outside for walks four or five times a day, every day, regardless of the weather.

Will your family life change?

Will your present circumstances always remain the same? It's a sad fact, but divorce can happen, causing couples or family units to break up, and you should consider what would happen to your dog, i.e. whether one party could still care for him, or whether he could remain with the reduced family group. Maybe you are planning to start a family – the arrival of a new baby can cause disruption to even the most placid household, so be sure that you can still give your dog plenty of attention.

How old are you?
Are you retired or planning to retire in the near future? If you are senior in years, you have to consider whether you will be fit enough to look after a young dog. It may not be a problem initially, but a lot can happen in the 10 years of a dog's life and you might not be as sprightly then as you are now.

Cavalier puppies look so cute and appealing, but you should only buy one for the right reasons after giving due consideration to your lifestyle, work and family commitments.

Cavalier puppies need a well-balanced diet if they are to grow and thrive, as well as plenty of interesting toys to play with.

Of course, taking a dog for a walk is great exercise and there are proven health benefits to pet ownership, including lower stress levels and better mental agility. However, you should consider whether an older Cavalier – maybe a rehomed dog from a rescue centre – might suit you better than a boisterous puppy.

Do you travel?

Do you go away for long weekends, short breaks, holidays or business trips? You also have to be mindful of what to do with your dog when you go away.

Nowadays, there are many 'dog friendly' hotels, B & Bs and rented holiday accommodation which welcome families with dogs, but these are very popular and get booked up quickly. if you are planning to take your dog abroad, you will have to sign up to the PETS Travel Scheme whereby dogs can accompany their owners, as long as they have all the necessary vaccinations and blood tests beforehand, and the correct paperwork (the so-called 'pet passport'). Again, this needs to be planned well in advance – you cannot simply take your dog to the ferry terminal or airport and say 'He's with us'. If he is not going on holiday with you, he needs to be boarded at suitable commercial boarding kennels, or you will need the services of a dog-sitter, who is CRB checked, whether this is a friend or someone offering a professional dog sitting service.

Acquiring your puppy

Having decided that you want to get a puppy and your work, lifestyle, home and family commitments make dog ownership possible, where do you start looking? Some people head for the high street, but buying a puppy from a pet shop or a commercial dealer should be avoided at all costs – and not just financial ones. That is not to say that all pet shops are bad – although nowadays there aren't many that sell puppies – nor that all commercial breeders are puppy farmers who exist only to mass produce 'cash crop' breeds, which includes the Cavalier along with other popular family breeds such as Labradors, Golden Retrievers and Staffordshire Bull Terriers.

Advertisements

There is no shortage of advertisements for puppies of any breed in your local newspapers, advertising papers and magazines, and there may be cards in a local newsagent's window, advertising puppies for sale. There are thousands of online advertisements, too, but,

generally, it is best to avoid these. Some breeders do advertise single breeds for sale and may be perfectly reputable, but avoid any breeder or establishment that offers multiple breeds for sale, as this may be a puppy farm, where 'cash crop' breeds are bred intensively. Puppies from such places often tend to be sickly and ill socialized.

Also, avoid dealing with anyone who says they will meet you at a motorway service station to deliver a puppy to you. Needless to say, avoid dealing with 'the man in the pub' who offers you a pedigree puppy. At best, it is most likely stolen; at worst, it will have been bred by a 'backstreet breeder' (a small-scale puppy farmer, in effect) and may have serious welfare problems. You will not get a good pedigree Cavalier puppy cheaply. By buying from puppy farms, 'men in pubs' and backstreet breeders, you are simply encouraging the over-production of unsocialized dogs with serious welfare problems.

Note: Sometimes local dog training clubs or veterinary surgeries will have details of a reputable breeder who has a litter of puppies and may be able to put you in touch with them.

Breeders

The best place to buy your Cavalier puppy will be from a reputable breeder, who is an enthusiast and has a great deal of experience with the breed and will probably exhibit Cavaliers frequently at dog shows. However, even amongst specialist breeders there will be the good and the not so good, so you need to do some research before making a decision on which dog to buy from whom. Begin by checking out the advertisements in the weekly specialist canine newspapers – *Our Dogs* and *Dog World* in the UK.

The Kennel Club is another good starting point as they will direct you to local Cavalier Clubs in your area as well as nationally. Log on to the Kennel Club website for more details (see page 126). The breed clubs can supply you with a list of breeders, but don't feel that you have to 'go local' to get the puppy you're after – be prepared to put yourself out and travel if you want the best.

Quiz the breeder

The next step is to check through the list of likely breeders and then telephone or e-mail them to get more information.

When buying a puppy, always make sure that you see the mother as well as the pups, preferably in the breeder's own home.

Ask them which colours they breed and whether they have any puppies available. Many breeders only have a litter or two a year, so you may have to be prepared to wait for a puppy from a particular breeder. Find out at what age their puppies are sold – some good breeders will not let a puppy leave their home under 12 weeks of age, whereas others may sell them as young as seven or eight weeks. Ask about the puppy's diet and what their adult Cavaliers eat.

Crucially, it's not just a matter of how much a puppy will cost you and when he will be available but also how healthy he and his parents are. It's a sad fact that many dog breeds suffer from a range of hereditary conditions, although since the introduction of the Kennel Club's hereditary diseases genetic screening process some years ago, some of the 'typical' inherited diseases have been greatly reduced in many breeds. Cavaliers have been known to suffer from heart problems and should be bred only from parents that are health tested annually. Only by buying a pup from such parents will you be able to feel reasonably secure that he is healthy.

Ask the breeder whether they health test their dogs and can produce the necessary veterinary paperwork to back this up. If they prevaricate or don't want to proceed on this basis, go elsewhere to another breeder. For more information on which hereditary conditions affect Cavaliers, turn to page 100.

Puppies need to play together and interact. It is all a vital part of their early socialization process and learning about the world.

When you go the breeder's house to view a litter of Cavalier puppies and choose the right one for you, make sure that you inspect their eyes, ears and teeth very carefully. If the puppies don't appear healthy, walk away.

Be prepared to be quizzed

A good breeder will ask you plenty of questions, too, so be prepared, don't be affronted and answer them honestly. A responsible breeder will want to make sure that you are a suitable potential owner and will ask questions about where you live, who shares your home, your working hours, other pets, previous dog ownership experience and why you want to own a Cavalier in particular.

Visit the breeder

The breeder might suggest that you visit a show and meet their show dogs. This gives you an opportunity to see how their dogs behave in public and react to other dogs and people. Arrange to visit their home or kennels, so you can view the mother and litter together, and check the conditions in which they are kept. It is not advisable to buy a puppy without seeing at least one parent beforehand and checking their health and temperament. It really is a case of 'what you see is what you get', and if you have any doubts about the parent dog, don't buy a puppy.

The puppies should be housed, ideally, in the breeder's home where they can be socialized and exposed to a range of people and household activities and noises. The surroundings should be clean and pleasant. If you are not happy with the puppies' environment and the way in which are are cared for, then walk away and find another breeder.

Observe the puppies

Watch the puppies carefully and how they react to you. When you approach a puppy, is he timid with his tail between his legs, or bold and 'up front', wagging his tail enthusiastically? Some puppies are naturally shy of strangers while others are more exuberant and curious, but a cowering, overly timid puppy is best avoided.

Check the puppies' health

Look at a puppy and judge whether he is lethargic or lively. Is he clean around his hindquarters? Do his ears, eyes and nose look clean and free of any discharge? A healthy puppy should have pink gums, and should not object to you taking a look in his mouth, although it's in a puppy's nature to have an exploratory nip with those sharp little new teeth. Are the gums overly pale? If so, the puppy may be ill or even suffering from anaemia. All puppies should have sweet, rather sickly breath – typical 'puppy breath' – so unless it smells particularly bad, don't worry too much about it.

Which sex?

Temperament-wise, there should be no difference between a Cavalier bitch and a dog, although some experts think that dogs are more territorial while bitches tend to be more temperamental. All dogs, just like humans, have their own individual personalities, irrespective of their sex. However, as a bitch matures, she will have regular seasons (when she is sexually receptive), and at these times, be careful when you are walking her in public places and protect her from the unwanted attentions of male dogs. Usually, this means that for two to three weeks she will be confined largely to home – and you have to be prepared for dealing with the bleeding that accompanies a season.

So unless you intend to breed from your bitch, the best thing is to have her spayed (neutered) as soon as she is old enough. Ask your vet for advice. Some breeders and vets recommend that you allow her to have one clear season before she is neutered, whereas others maintain it makes no difference.

Spaying is a responsible option, not only to avoid any unwanted litters but

Cavaliers are very sociable dogs, especially with their littermates. Watch the puppies to see how they interact with each other.

also from a health point of view, as un-spayed bitches, especially older ones, can sometimes get infections, such as pyometra, which is a potentially life-threatening condition.

Paperwork

When you decide to go ahead and buy a puppy, your breeder should provide you with a proper pedigree certificate for him, listing his parents, grandparents, great-grandparents, etc., as well as his Kennel Club registration document. They will be able to advise you on

having it transferred into your name once you become the dog's owner.

At the time of collection, you should receive a contract of sale, which should include a 'buy back' agreement clause, whereby the breeder agrees to take the puppy back if he is found to be suffering from any serious health problem within a reasonable period of time following the sale. Read the contract carefully to make sure this is included.

A good-quality chewing toy will help your Cavalier puppy to develop strong, healthy teeth as well as alleviating teething pain.

Ask the breeder what arrangements they have made, if any, about your puppy's vaccinations (see page 103). If he is being sold at over nine weeks of age, then the breeder should have initiated at least one of the two essential inoculations against infectious diseases. The puppy will need his second inoculation at around 11 weeks, which, most likely, will be your responsibility. Similarly, he should have been 'wormed', i.e. treated against worms and other parasites (see page 106), at least once or twice before coming to live with you. You should also ask the breeder about

These Cavalier puppies are happy in a secure outdoor pen in the garden, equipped with a water bowl, where they can play in safety while you are busy doing other things.

tests carried out for genetic problems within the breed (see page 100).

A good breeder should include puppy insurance as part of the sale package. This usually provides cover for any health problems and other eventualities covered in the policy during the first six weeks from point of sale. After this you must make your own arrangements, either with the same pet insurance company or another of your choice.

Preparing for your puppy

You now need to give some thought to preparing for your new puppy's arrival. You will need to buy some essential items, including the following:

- A bed or basket
- Bedding or blankets
- Food and water bowls
- Suitable food (which the breeder will advise you about)
- A collar and lead
- Some suitable toys, with no small parts that can be swallowed
- Some chews (puppy-sized) to help prevent damage to furniture or slippers
- A dog pen, or crate, can be a useful investment and will be your dog's 'own place', not so much for confinement as a safe area where he can reside and not get under your feet if you are busy and moving things around. Equally, it's a place of solitude for him.

Puppy-friendly home

You will also need to make sure that your house and garden are puppy-friendly. In the house, check the following:

- There are no small areas into which a puppy could crawl and get stuck
- No electrical wires are lying around – puppies like chewing them, so invest in some cable protectors (available from DIY and electrical stores) to tidy away TV and other electrical appliance wires
- Children's toys and small ornaments are out of reach, as a puppy likes nothing better than to chew things, and they could cause severe health problems if swallowed
- Cupboard doors should always shut securely, especially those containing sharp items or cleaning materials
- Child gates or special dog gates should be fitted in doorways or at the top or bottom of stairs; attach some strong wire mesh to the gate to prevent the puppy sticking his head between the bars and getting stuck.

You also need to survey your garden and make it escape proof. Check for the following:

- There should be no holes or obvious gaps in fences
- Garden gates shut properly and there is not sufficient space underneath for a puppy to squeeze through and escape
- If you have a garden pond, put a stout wire fence around it or strong netting over the top to prevent a puppy falling in
- There are no poisonous plants that your puppy could eat
- Weedkillers, slug pellets and other chemicals are securely locked away out of reach.

Contact the vet

Book an appointment for your puppy's vaccinations and health check. You may also wish to check out puppy training classes, which are organized by local clubs. Some veterinary surgeries also organize 'puppy parties' where puppies can meet each other and get used to other dogs and people.

Collecting your puppy

Finally, the big day will dawn and you will have to go to the breeder to collect your puppy. Take some towels and kitchen roll with you in case the puppy is stressed or unused to car travel and is sick. A water bowl and bottle of water will be necessary on a long journey as the puppy may be thirsty. If possible, take someone with you to collect the puppy, so that one of you can nurse him while the other drives.

When you arrive at the breeders, make sure the puppy you chose on your last visit is still fit and healthy, and then check the paperwork over. The breeder

A large, spacious outdoor run with a paved or concrete floor, which is totally secure, is an ideal area for several Cavaliers to exercise in.

should provide all the documents you need (see page 32), plus a diet sheet and two to three days' supply of the puppy's usual food. Once you have paid the breeder, it's time to take your puppy home. Some breeders even supply a 'puppy pack', which includes toys and maybe a blanket on which he and his mother have slept in order to provide a reassuring, familiar scent.

Make sure you keep a good hold of your puppy on the journey home. You can cuddle him on your lap or place him in a suitable carrier to keep him safe. Remember to reassure him as much as he needs, always talking quietly and in a friendly tone of voice, without overdoing the attention and making him anxious or over-excited. If you can, put a puppy collar (and lead) on him during the journey home, not to walk him – that comes later – but as part of the all-important process of getting him used to a collar and lead for his later training.

If you use public transport rather than driving him home in a car, avoid letting any other passengers touch your puppy. Of course, people will want to stroke him and make a fuss of him, but although it's good socialization it may also be quite stressful.

Arriving at home

When you bring your puppy home, it's important that you try to look at things from his point of view. He is just a few weeks old, and all he will have known are his mother and siblings, their puppy pen and the immediate area of the breeder's home in which they have been kept. Now he is on his own, with human beings he does not recognize by smell or sight, in a strange, new house. It's a traumatic experience for a young dog, so do not expect instant bonding. On the contrary, it is quite likely that he will be anxious, even frightened, in his new and unfamiliar surroundings.

The first thing you need to do as soon as you get out of the car is to take him into the garden and encourage him to urinate and/or defecate. When he performs, praise him lavishly and make

Toilet train your puppy early on. Start taking him out in the garden for this purpose as soon as you arrive home. Never shut him outside by himself. It is important to go with him and to encourage and praise him.

a fuss of him. Do not stop en route in lay-bys as these can be places of infection where countless other dogs have been. Until he has completed his course of vaccinations, your puppy cannot be put down in a public place.

The last thing your puppy needs is to be pitched into a house full of your friends and neighbours all descending at once to meet the new arrival, even if they are being friendly and just wanting to pet him. Just take things calmly and slowly; let the puppy explore the rooms you make available to him, such as the living room and kitchen. Show him his bed or basket; if the breeder has given you a blanket, put it in his bed along with his other bedding. Indicate where

Playtime together in the garden can also be used for some light training, such as learning to retrieve and give up a toy or item on command. When your puppy does this, always be sure to praise and reward him.

his food and water bowls are (ideally, these should not be situated too far away from his bed). Show him the back door, so that he can ask to be let out into the garden to toilet (which he will eventually learn to do).

All the time, talk to him gently, using his name. This has a practical purpose, as he needs to associate with his name and respond to it. Never shout or scold your puppy while using his name as an admonishment, or he will associate his name with something bad.

Bedtime

Puppies are, of course, babies, so they tire very easily. One minute they may be playing madly; the next, they may be sound asleep. So when your puppy has explored your house, maybe had a little bit to eat and hopefully, gone outside to toilet, encourage him to use his new bed. Again, do not shout or get impatient if he climbs out of his bed; if he flops down to sleep somewhere else, gently pick him up and put him in his own bed, so that he gets used to it.

One trick to help settle him down to sleep is to put an old clock in his bed, perhaps wrapped in a blanket. The ticking will remind him of his mother's heartbeat and reassure him. As he gets older and more confident, you will be able to remove the clock without causing him any upset. Sometimes keeping a radio switched on nearby (but not too loud) will help to reassure him further.

The first night

Expect your puppy to be fretful on his first night – he will be alone for the first time in a strange house. You could leave a small nightlight on in the kitchen or the room where he sleeps for the first few nights. Some owners don't mind having a dog in their bedroom, so if you want to take your puppy up to bed with you that's fine – but make him sleep in his own bed, not on yours. Not only is it safer – a fall from a bed could injure a small puppy – but it also gives the dog

the wrong message to allow him to sleep on your bed, as it elevates him mentally in his perceived 'pack hierarchy'. Your dog is lower than you in the pack – you are the pack leader – so he should expect to sleep in his own bed, not in yours.

From Day One, it is important to 'think dog'. Your Cavalier puppy is not a human being; he is a dog and he thinks like one and needs to be treated like one, so he won't feel rejected or upset if you don't allow him on your bed (or on the furniture). It will be more of a comfort to him to receive clear signals from his pack leader about his proper place in the family hierarchy.

A puppy crate (pen) will help your Cavalier puppy feel secure and will also give him his own special place to sleep and relax in.

Feeding your puppy

Puppies of eight to twelve weeks of age need four or five meals a day. It is best to ask the breeder for advice about diet before you buy your puppy, and they will usually give you a little of the food the puppy has been accustomed to eating. There are many good complete diets now available, some of which are aimed specifically at puppies.

A milk feed is a useful supplement to help provide extra calcium for the puppy's developing bones, but make sure it is a specially formulated mixture for puppies, and not cow's milk, which will not have all the necessary nutrients he needs and can cause diarrhoea.

At four to six months of age, the number of meals can be reduced to three per day, and at around nine to eleven months your puppy can be fed just once or twice a day.

There is a vast range of different dog foods to choose from, including 'complete' mixes, canned meat and pouches, as well as dry puppy 'mixers'. Some people eschew commercially

Mealtimes are very important. Young Cavalier puppies need to eat three or four times a day, depending on their age.

produced dog food altogether and prefer to feed their dog on a natural diet of fresh meat, bones and fish which, of course, is what dogs used to be fed on long before commercial dog food was invented. It is very much a matter of personal preference and of what suits your dog and provides all his dietary needs. Do some research – ask your vet, breeders and other dog owners, and read up on canine nutrition until you find what is best for you and your dog.

If you are feeding commercial puppy food, be sure to follow the instructions on the packet on how much to feed and how frequently. If you opt for a more natural diet, check with experienced dog owners and nutritionists first to ascertain just how much food you should be giving your growing puppy.

Supplementing the diet

Vitamins and other supplements may be added to your puppy's diet, but always follow the directions closely, particularly with regard to your puppy's age and breed. However, he may not need any supplements if he is fed a carefully prepared, balanced diet. If you have any queries about your dog's diet, contact the breeder or consult your vet.

House-training

The Cavalier is an intelligent dog and one of the easiest breeds to house train. You need to start house training your puppy straight away, as soon as you bring him home. However, you must be prepared to find puddles of urine and other little '*messages*' on your floor from time to time. If this happens, do NOT shout at the puppy or, worse, rub his nose in the offending mess. Simply pick him up or direct him to the door, put him outside and encourage him to urinate or defecate outdoors. Once he has done so, give him plenty of praise and make a fuss of him.

Very soon the lesson will be learned and, if a routine is followed whereby the puppy is always let out after he has eaten, had a drink, woken up from a sleep, had a boisterous game, etc., he will soon learn what is required of him. Later

Dogs sometimes eat grass, which acts as a kind of natural medicine for upset tummies.

on, as he gets older, he will let you know himself when he wants to go outside.

It is always a good idea to spread some old newspapers out on the kitchen floor in case your puppy has an accident – it saves a lot of mopping up. Over the course of a few days, gradually reduce the amount of newspapers until they | are only placed by the backdoor, which will help reinforce the message that the door equals 'outside' and 'outside' equals toilet. In time, however, you won't need to do this as your Cavalier will hopefully be fully house trained.

Some people place their puppy's bed and some newspapers in a dog crate or a child's playpen. As well as giving a puppy a quiet relaxing place of his own, this can also help with house-training. Dogs don't like making a mess near their sleeping area, so this will reinforce the message that the best place for your puppy to go is outdoors.

Finally, if you do still have the odd accident, then buy some strong odour eliminator (non-toxic, of course) to help get rid of any lingering smells after cleaning up the mess. This will help to prevent your puppy associating any 'no-go' area with toileting functions.

Exercise

Even young puppies need regular exercise, although this should not entail long walks, as their growing bones could get damaged by over use. Until your puppy finishes his course of vaccinations (see page 103), just play games with him and let him explore your garden. Now is a good time to get him used to wearing

Vaccinations

All dogs need to be vaccinated against distemper, parvovirus, hepatitis and leptospirosis. In some countries, they also need to be inoculated against rabies. In the UK, they will require anti-rabies vaccination if they are due to travel overseas. These diseases are all highly contagious and can prove fatal, so it is in your interest to undertake this precaution.

Inoculations are not generally very expensive and are easily arranged through your vet. It is also advisable to vaccinate your dog against kennel cough, which is particularly important if he is going to spend time with a lot of other dogs, such as in boarding kennels when you go away on holiday, at shows or in training classes.

Your new puppy will need his first inoculations at around eight to nine weeks of age, with a second bout around three weeks later. Vaccinations need to be 'boostered' at regular intervals (see page 103) in order to maintain the correct level of immunity in the dog's body. You should ask your vet for advice on this. Nowadays, as the efficiency of vaccines has gradually improved, booster vaccinations tend to be carried out bi-annually, although you will find that some vets still favour annual boosters.

a collar for short periods. When he is accustomed to it and no longer seems to notice it, he can wear it all the time. Similarly, attach a lead to it for a few minutes and take him for a little walk round the garden, just to get him used to the idea.

A week after he has been fully vaccinated, you can take him out to get him acclimatized to the world. Young puppies do not need long walks – their growing bones could even get damaged by overuse. Let your dog walk at his own pace in the park or a similar place, so he gets accustomed to wearing a lead for longer periods. He should soon begin to develop a sense of his local environment and build up a picture of the place through sights and, more importantly, smells. As he grows stronger and gets older, you can take him out more often and for longer distances.

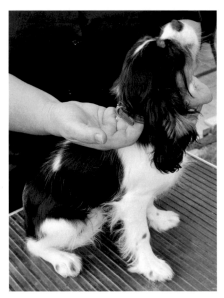

Put a soft collar on your puppy, but always make sure you can insert three fingers.

Wearing a collar and lead for short periods, your puppy will get used to wearing them, which will help immensely with his training.

Socialization

Socializing your puppy should begin very early on. He may seem a cute little ball of fluff but he thinks and acts like a dog. He needs to be aware of his place in the family pack and know what is expected of him, and it is important to make this clear and not to send mixed messages. This does not mean that you can't show him affection, which is vital to gain his trust. Just teach him what the boundaries are and establish some ground rules. For instance, he can grab and chew his toys but not your shoes; he can eat his food, but not steal yours from your plate; he can play with your family, but on your terms and when you say he can do so.

It is your job, as pack leader, to decide what is permissible and what behaviour is not acceptable. Praise him when he behaves well and responds in the required way, and be careful not to encourage or reinforce bad behaviour. He may seem sweet jumping up at your family and friends while he is a puppy, but this will not be acceptable when he is older, so stop this unwanted behaviour now.

Meeting people and going out

It goes without saying that your Cavalier should not be afraid of people, nor show aggression to strangers. This can easily be achieved by a process of carefully introducing your puppy to new people and letting him get accustomed to being

A firm 'No' will teach your Cavalier puppy not to indulge in unacceptable or potentially dangerous behaviour. However, be sure to always reward good behaviour with praise, tasty treats and playtime.

Children and puppies enjoy playing together, but make sure that you supervise them to ensure that it does not get too rough. Most young puppies love to play-bite.

When taking your Cavalier puppy for a walk, let him meet new people and thus become better socialized. It is also a good opportunity for him to meet other older dogs.

talked to and stroked by humans. In fact, the more people he meets and the more situations he experiences, the better he will be able to cope with going to new places. You can help this process by taking your puppy with you to as many places as possible (after his course of vaccinations, of course). He needs to experience traffic, public transport, and being in a range of public places, etc.

Cavaliers are naturally gregarious and they seldom show aggression to each other.

Meeting other dogs and animals

Your puppy will also need to get used to other dogs, so enlist the help of a friend who has a dog that is trustworthy around other dogs and introduce your puppy to their dog. Always be on hand to supervise such introductions and be ready to intervene if necessary. Puppies can be a bit over-exuberant and nip in playfulness – most older dogs realize this and will not over-react, although there may be some warning growls. A younger dog should submit to an older dog; this is natural and will help your puppy to define his place in the great scheme of things. If wished, you can restrain both dogs by leads, so that they can be pulled away from each other if it is necessary. Puppy socialization classes run by dog training groups are also helpful because your puppy needs to learn not to just run up to any dog – or person – he sees.

The same principles apply to any other dogs or pets you have at home. Introduce them in carefully supervised conditions. Cats tend to dispense short, sharp justice with a jab of their claws and a warning hiss – a lesson that your Cavalier puppy will quickly learn.

Visiting the vet

Some dogs dislike going to the vet – perhaps not surprisingly, because the vet may invariably become associated in the dog's mind with pain, whether from illness or injections. Therefore it is a very important aspect of your puppy's training to take him to the veterinary surgery occasionally for a check up or even just for a visit, so he comes to realize that the vet's surgery is not a threatening place and that the vet is really a nice person.

Grooming

Another routine to introduce from an early age is grooming. From the first week in your home, get your puppy accustomed to being handled and groomed. All he needs is a quick brush and teasing out any tangles or matted fur with a comb – be gentle and don't hurt him. Use these sessions as a time for getting to know each other better and bonding. He will soon come to enjoy them and you won't have problems grooming him when he is older.

These times together are also a good opportunity to check your puppy over and make sure there are no warning signs of future health problems. Check his ears, eyes and mouth. Part his coat and look for any unusual lumps or bumps and signs of fleas.

Grooming is also a good way of training your puppy to sit and stay still patiently and to get used to being handled by you.

Chapter 3
The adult Cavalier

As your Cavalier puppy grows into adolescence and adulthood, he should have integrated seamlessly into your family and be the source of much joy for you all. However, as with children growing up, so too must you be aware of what is required for the daily care and welfare of your adult dog.

He should have already learned his position in the family pack, be toilet trained and well socialized. He should also be trained to walk on the lead and respond to basic commands (see page 68). In short, you should have a well-balanced and happy dog.

Feeding

By the time your Cavalier is an adult (around 12 months), he will only need one or two meals a day. All dogs are omnivores, which means that they eat both meat and other food, so they can be fed mixer, cereals, pasta, rice and vegetables as well as meat.

Home-cooked food

In recent years, there has been a backlash against commercial, prepared dog foods and a move towards more 'natural' diets, including raw meaty bones, fish and home-prepared food. There is nothing wrong with this, but it can be time-consuming, so if you decide to go down this route, make sure you have enough time to prepare and cook your dog's food and be careful to get the balance of protein, minerals and vitamins right. Your vet should be able to advise you.

Commercial food

There is a vast range of commercially produced pet foods on the market, some of it better than others. The sensible option is to provide your Cavalier with one 'wet' meal (i.e. canned food) per day as well as one dry food meal.

Alternatively, you can feed him a 'complete' diet, which usually comes in dry form and is designed to provide all of a dog's dietary requirements. Some complete foods need to be soaked in water for half an hour before feeding to your dog, so always be sure to follow the instructions carefully. If dry food is given, Breeders and vets sometimes recommend adding a small amount of raw chopped vegetables to one of the

Your little Cavalier puppy will soon grow into a healthy adult dog, but he will still love to play with you and will be very affectionate.

two daily meals if dry food is fed to a dog. Follow the recommended feeding amounts as advised by the manufacturer.

Supplements

Vitamins and calcium supplements do not need to be added to complete diets, although, for the older dog, preparations that give relief to stiff joints and general aches and pains can be mixed with the complete food to make sure the dog takes them – the same rule will apply to some medication.

Treats and titbits

There's nothing wrong with a titbit (a small scrap of your own food) now and again or a treat. In fact, treats are very useful for training your dog, and many are available in supermarkets and pet shops. Do remember, however, that all treats should only be offered occasionally and then as a reward to reinforce good behaviour. If you always make your dog work for a treat, by responding to a simple command, such as sitting or fetching a toy, he will quickly learn that he has to do something to earn a reward, and this will assist his training.

Avoid giving your dog titbits just because he is begging and looking appealing. This only leads to problem behaviour in the future and it can be

A snood will help keep your Cavalier's ears from dangling into his food while he eats. You will find that this is especially useful on show days when you want him to look his best.

Playing games in the garden and chasing a ball will help to exercise your dog as well as being an enjoyable, relaxing time together.

annoying. You can prevent this by ignoring him when he begs for food, especially when you are eating.

Exercise

Naturally, being lively dogs, Cavaliers need exercising every day, including at least one walk, whatever the weather. Make sure that the distance you cover is within your dog's capability. Indeed, most dogs enjoy two or three walks a day, or even more. An elderly dog will not need to go for as many walks as a younger, fitter one, and when he does go out, he will be a lot slower, so you need to make allowances for this.

For elderly owners, who may not be so sprightly themselves, some play and retrieve games with their Cavalier in the garden will help exercise both of them.

When your dog comes back to you in the retrieve or on command, welcome him enthusiastically and give him a tasty treat.

If you have a younger dog, who is very energetic and needs plenty of exercise, you may have to arrange for someone else to walk him for you, whether it's a family member, friend or paid dog walker. Some animal charities organize voluntary dog walking services for elderly or incapacitated owners.

Information gathering

Dogs use their walks constructively to find out more about their locality. Their noses are infinitely more sensitive than ours – estimated to be 1,000 times more sensitive. Dogs have more than 220 million olfactory receptors in their nose, whereas humans have only 5 million. Because of this keen sense of smell, dogs are used to locate everything from drugs, firearms and explosives to human beings. Just by sniffing other dogs or the urine traces that they leave behind them, your Cavalier can build up a clear mental image of them, so going out for regular walks enables him to catch up with all the local canine gossip.

Responsible ownership

Finally, don't forget that it's responsible pet ownership as well as the law to 'clean up' after your dog. There are plenty of special devices available on the market, but nothing beats a small plastic bag. A top tip is to purchase a supply of nappy sacks for picking up – not only are they relatively cheap but they are also scented. Keep one in your pocket when you walk your dog. Always dispose of the used bags responsibly – ideally in a specially designated bin for this purpose.

Grooming

Your Cavalier needs regular grooming, but this need not be as daunting as it sounds. It is a learning process for both you and your dog. Generally, Cavaliers are very clean dogs, but they do get gloriously dirty at times, so give your dog a quick brush and comb or towel dry after a walk in the rain or a run in the countryside.

Grooming equipment

You will need to purchase a few items of grooming equipment to look after your dog's coat and keep it in good condition as well as to keep him generally healthy, for the grooming process encompasses other areas, too. You will need:
- A stiff brush – natural bristles are best
- A strong comb, ideally with medium and fine teeth combined
- A de-matting comb
- A grooming mitt (glove)
- A toothbrush
- A de-scaler (optional), rather like the one a dentist uses
- Strong dog nail clippers.

If you want to be very organized or are planning to show your dog, you could also purchase a special grooming table, which is suitable for small dogs, although any solid table will suffice. The surface needs to be non-slip, so if you are using an ordinary table, a rubber car mat or cut-off piece of carpet can be used.

The coat

If you started getting your Cavalier accustomed to gentle grooming while he was a puppy (see page 45), he will not be difficult to groom as an adult. Simply brushing an adult's long fur will only take care of the surface by removing any dirt, leaves and loose hairs.

You will need to use a comb to reach the dense undercoat, which helps keep the dog's skin well aerated. A de-matting comb may look like a vicious, sharp instrument, but it breaks up stubborn

A special grooming table will make grooming your dog easier, especially if you show him.

knots in the fur very well. Always be gentle and take care not to tug hard on any tangles and matts, as this will hurt your dog and will put him off being groomed. You want your dog to enjoy the process – this is a time when you can get to know each other.

At the end, run the comb all over his body to remove any remaining loose fur and add extra shine to his coat.

1 Use a slicker brush on your Cavalier's ears to gently remove any knots and burrs that may accumulate in the long hair.

2 Next comb through the hair on the dog's ears with a fine comb, using first the thicker and then the finer edge.

3 Groom the 'bib' at the front of the chest under the head. Gently comb through, teasing out any tangles.

4 The next stage is to comb through the leg feathering under the arms. Always be gentle and never pull sharply on the hair.

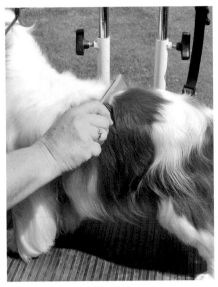

5 Remove dead hair and debris from the dog's back. Do this is with a fine comb, working from neck to tail.

6 Use a slicker brush on the back of the legs. If you find any knots, tease them out with your fingers before brushing.

7 You will also need to use the slicker on the dog's tail. This is another area where the long hair can get knotted and dirty.

8 Lastly, go over the dog again with a fine comb. This will loosen any dead hairs and give the coat a healthy shine.

9 If there are bad knots, use some grooming spray on those areas, especially behind the ears, to make them easier to comb.

10 After spraying the problem areas in the coat, you can gently ease out any knots and matted hair with a fine comb.

Eyes

Your Cavalier's eyes will also need your attention – all dogs get some occasional discharge from their eyes but the bulbous eyes and flattish faces of Cavaliers often lead to what is called 'guttering' whereby dirt accumulates on each side of their muzzle. Use a piece of cotton wool, which has been soaked in warm water or a specially formulated cleanser from a good pet store, and gently wipe around the eye and through the 'gutters', removing any discharge. Use a dry piece of cotton wool to dry the area around the eye. As with ear cleaning, always use one piece of cotton wool per eye.

Clean under the dog's eyes with some cotton wool, which has been soaked in warm water, eye cleaner or witch hazel.

Ears

Your dog's ears are all-important, and they need not only regular combing and brushing but also some internal attention to prevent the build up of

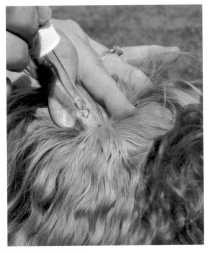

You can use a special cleaning fluid to keep your Cavalier's long ears clean and healthy. Administer it with a pipette.

dirt and wax and check for possible infections and discharges. The best way to do this is not to poke around with a cotton bud but to use a small piece of cotton wool, soaked in proper ear cleaning fluid (available from your vet or pet store). Gently move the cotton wool around the ear canal – never pushing or prodding too deeply – to pick up any dirt and excess wax. Always use a separate piece of cotton wool for each ear. The outside of the ears can be brushed and combed in the usual way, but don't tug hard on any tangles – tease them out gently. Cavaliers' ears can easily get knotted and act as a repository for twigs, sticky bits of food and other assorted debris.

After adding ear cleaning fluid or a little olive oil, massage the ear area gently. Your dog will probably enjoy this.

Alternatively, you can wipe round inside the ear with some cotton wool soaked in cleaning fluid or a little olive oil.

Dental care

A Cavalier's teeth are generally very clean and strong, but in older dogs, tartar can often build up and this is where a tooth scraper comes into play. This is a two-handed job, where someone needs to hold the dog's head whilst you gently but firmly scrape any tartar off his teeth, being careful not to catch his gums with the scraper. You can ask your vet to show you how to do this or, if you are not confident about attempting it yourself, ask them to do it for you.

As a general aid to keeping your dog's teeth clean and healthy, it is a good idea to buy a doggy toothbrush and special tooth paste (invariably meat flavoured, so that the dog won't object) and use this as regularly as it is needed – ideally, once a week when you groom him.

Nowadays, you can purchase special canine toothbrushes, such as these, with which to clean your Cavalier's teeth.

Squeeze a little meat-flavoured canine toothpaste on to the toothbrush. You don't need to use much to brush the teeth.

Reach right to your Cavalier's back teeth to give them a good scrub. If you do this gently and start at an early age, he will accept this.

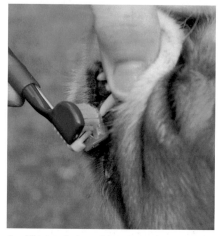

A stiffer-headed toothbrush can be used to pay attention to your Cavalier's front teeth. Always be gentle and careful not to hurt him.

Your Cavalier's claws need to be clipped regularly. With pale claws, such as these ones, it is relatively easy to see the 'quick'.

Claw care

Regular walking will keep your Cavalier's claws nicely honed down. However, if they are very sharp and they appear to be growing too long, they must be trimmed, or they will eventually curl over and cause the dog great discomfort. Carefully hold his leg straight and clip the excess length of

Trim the long tufts of fur from between your Cavalier's toes, as these can become knotted.

claw away with the clippers, being careful not to go too close to the dog's paw – cutting the quick of the nail is painful and causes a lot of bleeding. If your Cavalier has dark claws, it's even harder to see where the quick begins, so take extra care. If you are unsure of how to clip your dog's claws, ask an experienced owner to show you or simply get your vet to do it. To be successful, you must be careful and earn your dog's trust. It will also help to trim the fur between the pads of his paws, which will help prevent dirt and grit getting caught in the fur and causing your dog pain when he walks.

Clipping

Some owners like to clip their Cavalier's coat, but it is a specialist task which is best left initially to a professional dog groomer or to a more experienced owner who knows how to trim the fur correctly. Like everything else, it is a matter of learning and experience.

General health

Cavaliers are generally robust, healthy dogs, although, like any animal, they can suffer from a range of problems. In general care terms, there are some issues of which you should be aware.

Worming

All dogs are susceptible to parasitic worm infestations and should be treated regularly. Worming tablets are available 'over the counter' in supermarkets and pet shops, or from your vet who will have the most effective treatments. It is your duty as a responsible owner to worm your dog regularly to keep him in good health. Ask your vet for advice and to supply a suitable worming treatment for your dog (see page 106).

Fleas

It's an inescapable fact that even the cleanest of dogs can get fleas, usually from other dogs or simply from the

Bathing your dog

Every dog will need a bath now and again. If you are showing your Cavalier, this will be a regular event, but, even so, bathing is something your dog should get used to. It does not require much equipment – just some towels and a good-quality dog shampoo. There are lots of these on the market, including medicated coat colour specific and homeopathic brands, any of which are designed to kill fleas (see above). To bath your dog, do the following:

1 Put a few inches of lukewarm water into a bath, bowl or sink, and place a bath mat or car mat in the bottom to prevent your dog slipping.

2 Stand your dog in the water on the mat and wet his coat with lukewarm water, preferably from a showerhead.

3 Once the fur is soaked, work the shampoo into the coat, right down to the skin, paying close attention to the ears, tail and rear end. Give the paws a good lathering, too, working in between the toes and under the claws to remove any stubborn bits of dirt and debris that can accumulate there. Be careful not to get shampoo in your dog's eyes or ears.

4 When the dog is well lathered, rinse the shampoo out thoroughly with clean, lukewarm water.

5 When you are satisfied that he is really clean, lift the dog out of the bath and dry him off with a towel as far as possible. Every dog will want to shake himself after being wet, so be prepared for this before you dry him. Alternatively, you can use a hairdryer, but do be careful not to let it get too hot or hold it too close to the dog. Whichever method you choose, make sure your Cavalier does not get too cold in the meantime.

6 When the fur has fully dried, simply give it a brushing with a brush and grooming mitt to remove any remaining loose hairs.

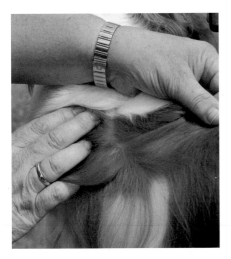

Examine your dog regularly for tell-tale signs of fleas. When applying the 'spot on' type of flea drops, make sure you part your dog's fur carefully to expose the bare skin beneath.

Apply the flea drops to the exposed area of skin, usually on the neck behind the head so that the dog cannot lick it. The drops will then be absorbed more easily.

environment. Fleas survive in the dog's fur and live by sucking blood through his skin. A dog with fleas invariably draws notice to the fact by scratching frequently and rolling over to relieve the irritation of these little vampire-like insects. Fleas are the Olympic athletes of the insect world and they can leap surprisingly long distances – from your Cavalier's body onto other dogs or anywhere in your house where they lay their eggs. They are remarkably robust and their eggs and pupae can lie dormant in carpets and soft furnishings for months, even if the adult fleas have been eradicated by flea spray.

Fleas and tapeworms have a symbiotic parasitical role. As well as worming your Cavalier regularly, it is essential to administer a good-quality flea treatment, usually in the form of a spray or 'drop

on' pipette-type dispenser, which is absorbed directly into the dog's body through the skin of his neck.

Garlic tablets can help keep your dog flea-free, as fleas do not like the taste of the garlic in the dog's skin. However, they are a preventative aid rather than a treatment. For more information on fleas and how to prevent them, see page 104.

Security

Dog identification is both a matter of responsible dog ownership and the law. It always makes sense to ensure that your dog can be properly identified and returned to you should he stray from home, get lost or, worse, be stolen and subsequently sold on to someone.

Under the UK Control of Dogs Act 1992 every dog, while in a public place, must wear a collar with the name and

Your dog should always wear a collar, and this should carry an identity tag with your name and address or phone number clearly visible.

Microchipping

Sadly, some dogs are destroyed because their owners cannot be found and they cannot be rehomed. However, if a dog is microchipped with his own unique identification number registered on a national database, owners can be traced very quickly and reunited with their pets.

A microchip is a small, inert silicon chip transmitter, housed in bicompatible glass, made from soda lime, just slightly larger than a grain of rice, which is inserted into the skin at the back of a dog's neck between the shoulder blades. The procedure is usually carried out by a veterinary surgeon, veterinary nurse or a trained breeder, although many microchip companies and registries employ specially trained personnel.

The injection of the chip is not painful, and, once in place, the chip causes no discomfort, nor will the dog's bodily defences reject it as a foreign body. If the chip is inserted correctly, it will not move.

address (or telephone number) of his owner inscribed on it or on a disc which is attached to it. If a collar is not worn when out in a public place, the dog may even be seized by a dog warden and can be treated as a stray.

It is amazing how many people do not have adequate identification for their dogs, even when it is just a simple matter of just providing a collar and engraved disc. There are several methods of identification available and, in these days of increasing dog theft and even changes of the law regarding stray dogs, there are many good reasons to correctly ID your Cavalier.

A microchip can be easily and painlessly injected into your dog's skin. This can be done by your breeder or veterinary surgeon.

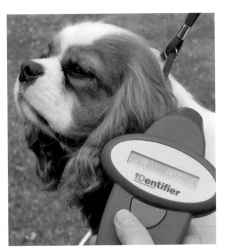

Once inserted, the microchip can be read by a special hand-held scanner which shows the chip's unique registration number.

The identification number, which is logged on a central database, can be updated at any point during the dog's life. When a special microchip scanner is passed over his shoulders, a signal activates the microchip and transmits back the unique ID number, which can be checked against registration records.

Tattooing

Tattooing your Cavalier's ear is another safeguard against straying and a visible deterrent to dog thieves. It is less hi-tech than microchipping but it has proved equally effective. The tattoo contains a unique registration number for your dog, which can be checked on the central dog tattoo database to find the details relating to him.

Tattoos do not fade over time and, if properly done by trained dog tattooists, do not smudge or cause pain to the dog when put in place via a clamp on the ear. As Cavaliers have very long fur inside their ears, the tattooist will have to shave some of it away, but it will grow back and the tattoo can be found by parting their fur. Tattoos are not as high-tech as microchips – or even the new 'sat nav' collars for tracking a dog if he strays – but they are effective and have been proven to reunite many a lost dog with his owner. For more information, see page 126.

Rescuing a Cavalier

You may consider taking on an adult Cavalier rather than acquiring a puppy. Some breeders occasionally have older dogs for sale, and these will have been socialized and trained, although they will, of course, need to get used to you, your family and your routine.

Breed rescues

These are another route to acquiring an older dog, and it is a sad fact that so many dogs end up unwanted for various reasons in breed rescues. They take the dogs and kennel them or place them with foster volunteers until suitable new homes can be found.

These societies provide an invaluable service, and nearly every breed club will operate some form of rescue. Check with a Cavalier Club whether they operate or can recommend a breed rescue organization. Alternatively, go on the Kennel Club's website for information.

The breed rescue staff will ask you some personal questions to determine whether you are a suitable owner before they will even consider you, so be

Most Cavaliers are adaptable dogs and even adult rescue dogs will usually settle in quite quickly into their new homes.

Some breed rescues do not sign over full ownership of the dog to you, but instead, you adopt it on a kind of leasing system. In any event, if you are unable to keep the dog for whatever reason, you will sign an agreement whereby he will be returned to the organization.

You will need to be mindful of the adopted dog's age and how this relates to the 'baggage' he may bring with him from his previous home. He may have been ill-treated, physically or mentally, and may be nervous, even defensive. The rescue centre should be able to tell you as much as they know about his background and offer advice on his care. If they don't volunteer this information, don't be afraid to ask. You need to know as much as possible before you commit yourself to caring for a rescue dog.

Settling in a rescue dog

The same settling-in rules apply for an adult dog as for a puppy – give him space and time to explore his new home, to find out where everything is and learn your new routine. Even some house-trained older dogs may have the odd accident due to stress before they settle down in their new home, so be prepared for this and on no account scold the dog. Instead, reward good behaviour. You both have to get used to each other.

Remember that your rescued Cavalier may have been mistreated by his previous owners or be traumatized by leaving his old home. It usually takes patience, time and, above all, a lot of love from you, before he will settle in to his new environment and accept his new family.

prepared for this. Usually they will want to know the details of your family circumstances, your daily routine and if there is someone at home to look after the dog as well as what sort of house you live in, whether it has a secure garden and, above all, your commitment to taking on a dog who has left his original home, or may even be on a second or third home.

If you are deemed to have answered their questions satisfactorily, you will receive a home visit from a volunteer, who will check out your house. Don't be offended by this – it is all part of ensuring that the rehomed dog's welfare is paramount.

The elderly Cavalier

Old age catches up with us all eventually and your Cavalier is no exception. From the age of eight, he is technically a 'veteran', and you should expect him to begin to slow down a little after he reaches this point. He may not be so active and may no longer need such long walks; he may be prone to old age conditions, such as joint stiffness, arthritis, failing eyesight and hearing. He may lose some of his teeth and, as dentures are not generally available for dogs, adjustments in his diet will be needed with a trend towards softer foodstuffs. Indeed, older dogs may need special diets so as not to put on excessive weight (especially as they take less exercise). An experienced owner of older dogs is your best source of information, as well as your vet, who will be able to give your 'oldie' regular health checks and whatever treatment he may need.

Some dogs age very gracefully, but be mindful of your Cavalier's advanced years and don't expect too much from him. Keep his daily life as calm and quiet as possible. That said, many older Cavaliers revel in having younger dogs around and whilst they enjoy their role as elder statesdog, they can still play hard and prove that there is life in the old dog yet!

Chapter 4

Training your dog

Cavaliers are affable, happy-go-lucky dogs, but always bear in mind that they are dogs, not little people. They don't think as humans do; they think as dogs. Dogs are essentially pack animals and a great deal of their behaviour is dictated by the basic, natural pack instinct. Even a single dog will look to his human owner as the nearest thing to a pack leader. It's when the boundaries of this relationship become blurred, and the dog is allowed to take liberties beyond his natural position in the pack hierarchy, that problems arise.

Of course, nobody wants to live with a misbehaved and bad-tempered dog. If nothing else, you have to consider the safety of your family, other people, dogs and pets. Good communication is key: you and your dog have to understand each other and also learn each other's language. You have to 'think dog', because that is how your Cavalier thinks. The essence of all communication and training is simple: you reward desired behaviour while correcting or ignoring undesirable behaviour.

Training guidelines

There are a few key points to remember when training your Cavalier:

- Keep training sessions short, especially with a puppy. Like children, they have a short attention span – 10 minutes is long enough for early sessions
- You can do basic training at any time, simply by working the training into your daily routine. Make your Cavalier sit and wait or just wait beside you before you feed him, or ask him to sit before you throw his ball, or a toy, for him to fetch. Your commands and the required actions will soon become fixed in his mind

A well-trained Cavalier is a happy dog and a joy to own. It is your responsibility as an owner to teach your dog good behaviour.

- Your commands must be clear and concise, so always use the same single word for one task. So 'Sit' means sit upright and 'Down' means lie down. However, if your Cavalier jumps up at you, then use a different word, such as 'Off'.
- Training sessions should be consistent, using repetition, praise and, above all, positive reinforcement. Be aware that punishment-based training leads to avoidance behaviour by a dog, whereas reward-based training is a 'fun' and encouraging method.
- Don't expect your Cavalier to grasp and learn everything immediately – give him time. He is a smart dog, so it won't take him long!

Separation training

One of the first training exercises you can carry out does not even involve the use of leads or collars – it is simply a matter of getting your puppy accustomed to spending some time on his own. Put him in one room, say, the kitchen, where his bed is located and then leave the room, perhaps closing the

Equipment

You don't need a lot of specialist equipment to train your dog but there are a few essential items that are worth buying.

- A suitable collar – NOT a choke chain! This is a very outmoded form of collar for a dog and does nothing to give you greater control of him. Equally, electric shock collars are NEVER to be used. Not only are they cruel, literally giving the dog an electric shock when he does something wrong, but they do nothing to reinforce lessons and can totally destroy a dog's trust in his owner. There are moves afoot to have such collars banned in the UK
- A good, strong lead – like collars, these come in a variety of materials, ranging from plastic to fabric or leather. Usually a good-quality lead (and collar) will be reflected in its price. Anything that looks too fancy with lots of adornments is not necessarily going to be useful to help train a dog. A puppy can have a softer collar, which can be replaced with a stouter, stronger one as he grows up
- A clicker – this is optional but if you do choose to use one (see below) make sure you keep it close to hand at all times. Only ever click with it when you need to as part of a training exercise
- Treats – use these to reward your dog when he does something right. Avoid chocolate or sweets; instead, use small dog biscuits, training chews that can be broken into an ideal size, or liver 'nibbles' which are available from good pet shops. Pieces of cheese or cut-up sausages are also very useful. Above all, don't overdo them – too many treats could make your Cavalier fat and, besides, if he does get full up, he won't feel like learning anything else.

door. Wait a couple of minutes and then go back into the room with minimal fuss. If he runs to greet you, make a fuss of him and then carry out some other task. Repeat the exercise, gradually extending the periods you are being absent from the room or the house, until he is comfortable with it. Of course, no dog should be left alone unattended for too long, but your Cavalier should be able to cope alone for five or six hours by the time he is a young adult. Never forget to leave a bowl of fresh drinking water if you are away for any length of time, and a chewy snack or bone will help him to pass the time pleasantly.

Teach your puppy his name

Teaching your puppy his name is the first step to successful training. Use his name a lot, always in a friendly tone of voice, but never when scolding him. Call him by name to give him a treat or a cuddle, and use his name when you feed him. Get him accustomed to realizing that nice things will happen to him when he hears his name and responds, and you will find that he will learn his name in a day or so.

Toys are a useful tool in training your puppy. He will enjoy chasing them and bringing them back to you for a tasty treat reward.

Coming when called

It is mind boggling how many dogs do not come back when their owners call them, especially as it is so easy to teach when they are young. Start early with your puppy to avoid problems later on. As an adult he can then be given a lot of freedom with walks off the lead in city parks or the countryside. When out for your first short walks together, let your puppy off the lead in a secure area.

Alternatively, you can commence training in the privacy and calm of your own garden where distractions should be minimal. The first and most important exercise is to teach your Cavalier to respond when called by his name.

Young puppies will follow their owners like ducklings trail after their mother and do not want to be left alone. Make a habit out of changing the direction you walk in without telling your puppy. Hide behind a bush or run away from your pup, calling his name. In no time at all, he will learn to keep his eyes on you and always follow you. Never wait for your puppy or run after him. He should keep his eyes on you, not the other way around. Call him frequently during walks just to praise him, and release him again. Keep this up throughout his life and coming when called will become second nature to him.

Teaching an adult

If your Cavalier is an older puppy or adult dog who already has an ingrained bad habit of not coming when called, try using an extendable lead or a long line for teaching training recalls.

I Attach a line to your dog's collar. Call him by name and if he does not come, tug at the lead and haul him in – but not too roughly – as you run backwards.

2 Praise him and give him a treat when he comes to you, then let him go again until he responds well enough for you to try it without the use of the lead or line. Repeat this over and over. Old dogs can learn new tricks, and the required response should become fixed in an older dog's mind eventually.

'Sit'

The command 'Sit' has many uses, and all dogs can learn it easily and quickly. There may be many occasions both around the house and when you are out and you need your dog to sit at your side. This is an important command to teach and you need to be confident that he will do as you ask and stay put.

1 Stand in front of your puppy on the lead and show him a tasty treat. Try to get him interested in it.

2 Tell him to 'Sit' as you raise it above his head. As his nose goes up, his bottom will go down and he will sit.

Be consistent

Make sure that you are consistent. Only say 'Sit' once, and if your Cavalier does not sit immediately, gently make him sit (as described above). Do not repeat the command as that will only teach the dog that he does not have to listen. Just use one word as a command, and don't say 'Sit down' as this will confuse him. 'Sit' should mean sitting down, whereas 'down' means lying down. Your puppy cannot do both at the same time – his default setting would be to do neither.

3 As soon as your puppy sits, praise him enthusiastically and give him the treat as a reward for his good behaviour.

'Down'

Use this command when you want your dog to lie down rather than sit. It is very useful for teaching your dog obedience and keeping him in a quiet and passive position if the situation demands it. Just practise the following steps.

I Standing in front of your puppy and holding his lead, ask him to 'Sit' as you have already taught him to do.

2 Show him a tasty treat and get him interested in it and let him smell it before you start lowering your hand.

3 Place your hand, with the treat in it, on the ground in front of him. Move the hand forwards, saying 'Down' firmly.

4 Your dog should naturally drop into the down position as he lowers himself to the ground to follow the treat.

5 Praise him once he is lying down and give him the treat immediately.

Persevere

Use one word only – 'Down', not 'Lie down'. Some stubborn dogs are not happy to lie down as it puts them in a submissive position, which makes them anxious. If this is the case with your puppy, you do need to persevere and, if necessary, firmly but gently push him into the down position. Even a stubborn dog will eventually defer to a consistently minded owner. Praise your Cavalier when he is lying down and relaxed, then say 'OK' or some other word as a 'release word', indicating he can now get up again. If you are consistent and use lots of praise, your dog will soon learn to drop down when given the command, although learning this usually takes a little longer than teaching the 'Sit' command.

'Stay'

This command is one of the most useful ones you will ever teach your Cavalier – or any other dog. Imagine that you are walking him on the lead and you need to bend down to pick up his mess. If you can tell him to sit and stay this will be easy – if he keeps moving around, it is much more difficult. In addition, should your dog ever run towards a busy road or any other danger, a well-trained 'Stay' command may save his life.

You can teach the 'Stay' in either a sitting, down or standing position, but it is easiest to start with a 'Sit' stay. As always, you must be consistent with your commands and do not vary them or you will confuse your Cavalier.

1 With your dog on a lead and standing in front of him, tell him to 'Sit'.

2 Now, showing him the flat of your hand as a visual stay signal, you must tell him very firmly to 'Stay'.

3 Take one step back away from him, repeating the word 'Stay' with your hand still raised.

4 If your Cavalier does not move, praise him lavishly and give him a treat.

Taking it further

Once your dog has understood what the 'Stay' command means, you can start staying away for slightly longer periods, and then taking two steps instead of one, and then gradually moving back even further, dropping the lead onto the floor. As long as you do not rush the exercise and you allow your dog to learn slowly over a period of time (usually a few weeks) he can be taught a reliable stay. In fact, it is possible to teach him to stay in one place even whilst you move out of sight.

To reinforce the lesson, once your Cavalier has learnt what 'Stay' means, you should go back frequently and feed him treats during the stay and then leave again, so that he learns that he is rewarded when staying and even if you come back he cannot jump up or move until you release him, by means of a simple, designated release word, such as 'OK'.

Walking on the lead

It may sound obvious that all dogs should be able to walk on the lead, but if you look around when you are out with your dog, you will probably see a lot of owners who are being pulled around by their pets, hardly even able to hold on to them. Worse, they may not have any control over their dogs, who will jump up at other people, which can be quite unnerving for strangers.

Walking a dog who pulls hard on the lead is not a pleasant experience, even with a small breed like a Cavalier, so you need to make sure that your dog walks nicely at your side to heel on a slack lead. Again, it is easiest to start this training with a puppy or young dog who has not developed bad habits.

Teaching a puppy

With a very young puppy, you will need to get him used to wearing a collar and lead before you even start lead walking. Use a soft fabric collar and lightweight lead. The first time you put it on him, he will scratch at the collar and try to get it off. Distract him by playing with him, and he will soon forget he is wearing it. Don't forget to add an engraved metal disc with your name, address and telephone number. It's a good idea to practise lead walking in your back garden or even in the house before you venture out for an actual walk.

Initially, it is usually best for the dog to walk on your left side whilst holding the lead in your left hand or holding it across your body in your right hand. This allows you greater control, with a significant part of the lead across your body.

Don't twist the lead around your hand or wrist as this reduces your control ability (and also hurts if your dog decides to pull). Keep one hand in the loop of the lead, with the other further down the lead for control. If you are left-handed, you may need to reverse the arrangement, but in any event, the dog should be on your left side.

You want him walking by your side, not dashing backwards and forwards in front of you, possibly tripping you up. A small puppy is unlikely to cause many problems if he pulls on the lead, but may be difficult to hold if he still does the same when he is an adult.

Stay in control

When going through doors or similar, the puppy should always follow you – he should never be in front – not only because you are pack leader but also to enable you to stay in control and on the look out for any 'unknown quantity' on the other side.

This enables you to make the necessary adjustments for your dog who is following you. Do not give him the opportunity to walk ahead of you – he should always walk only at your side or behind you. There is no need to use any command.

1 When you first attach a lead to his collar, your puppy will most likely not want to walk at all. If this happens, call him by name, encouraging him to come to you. Keep a titbit in your hand.

2 He will soon learn to follow you, but make sure that he does not pull. Hold the lead in your left hand, so he walks on your left side, and hide the titbit in your right hand.

3 If he pulls ahead, stop and say 'Heel', bringing him back to your left side. Praise him when he is in the right position beside you and set off again.

4 Have a slack lead and don't keep it too short, which will encourage the dog to pull. When he walks well beside you, give him a treat as a reward.

Teaching an adult dog

For an older dog who has already learnt to pull, there are various methods you can use to stop this bad habit.

1 You can simply stop walking as soon as your dog pulls and make him sit, so that eventually he will learn that he will get nowhere if he does pull.

2 You can change direction every time he starts to pull ahead.

3 A head collar – several different brands are available – can be extremely useful for an adult dog who pulls hard on the lead. It will enable you to control him with ease and will stop him pulling. Initially, your Cavalier will not like it and will try to remove it, but with praise and encouragement he will get used to wearing it. Compare this to how we can control large horses with head collars – it is the same technique as with dogs.

Busy places

In time, as your Cavalier gets used to walking on the lead, you will need to take him to places where there are lots of people – such as a busy street. To start with, carry him to reassure him as he gets used to the unfamiliar sights, sounds, smells and noises. As he grows more confident, however, let him walk on the pavement, but on a short lead and close to heel, so that he does not trip people up or get trodden on.

Remember, too, that very few shops and public buildings allow dogs inside unless they are assistance dogs. True, you could tie him up outside a shop whilst you are inside – it's all a good training to reduce anxiety separation behaviour, but it is not advisable in these times of increasing instances of dog theft. If you need to go into a shop, make sure you have a friend or family member with you who can stay outside with your dog. In any event, this is all good socialization training, because passers-by will want to stroke him and make a fuss of him. Training can be ongoing all the time.

Not jumping up

Few things can be so annoying as a dog who jumps up on people, especially if he has muddy paws or sharp claws. It may seem cute when he is a little puppy with dry paws but not when he is fully grown

Opposite: This well-trained Cavalier is happily walking to heel beside his owner.

Your Cavalier should learn early on not to jump up unless he is told to do so by you.

When your Cavalier is out for a walk on the lead and meets other dogs, he should be well behaved and sit when requested to do so.

and ruins your clothes. Never allow your puppy to jump up on you – just push him off gently and say a firm negative command, such as 'No'. When you greet your puppy, try to get down to his level, so he has no need to jump up to gain your attention.

With an adult Cavalier who jumps up, just turn your back on him and ignore him. Give him praise and your attention when he sits, along with a tasty treat to reward his good behaviour, and he will soon learn that it is far more rewarding not to jump up at people.

Treats and rewards

With all the basic training exercises featured above, a treat as a reward helps to reinforce the lesson in a positive way – along with plenty of praise given in a friendly, encouraging voice.

Over time, however, as your Cavalier grows older, the food treats can be withdrawn gradually. Practise a few lessons of 'Sit', 'Stay' and 'Come' (or other commands that suit your lifestyle) and only give a reward now and again, substituting praise and a pat. Eventually, you may be able to dispense with food

Opposite: This obedient, well-behaved Cavalier puppy is waiting in a sit stay for the next command from his owner.

treats altogether, although a little tasty treat now and again for rewarding good behaviour and being a good dog will never go amiss!

Clicker training

Many professional dog trainers use this method nowadays. Clicker training is a way of 'positive reinforcement training', which basically rewards the behaviours that we like instead of punishing the behaviours that we don't like.

The clicker itself is simply a small plastic box, containing a metal plate, which, when pressed, makes a 'click' sound. A dog will hear it very clearly and respond to it. When your Cavalier does as he is told, you 'click' the clicker and give him a treat. He will soon learn to associate the good behaviour with the 'click' and the forthcoming treat, and will learn to repeat the behaviour.

Clickers can help with our timing. By the time you have praised your Cavalier for performing the desired action, he may have stopped the positive behaviour and started doing something else. Our dogs do not have the mental reasoning to determine what they are being praised for, so they can sometimes receive a confusing, mixed signal.

Start training your dog

The clicker should be combined with small tasty treats, such as liver pieces or food sticks. When you begin clicker training, make sure that there are no distractions. Introduce your Cavalier to the clicker by showing it to him, then click it once and give him the treat. He does not have to do anything for his treat – he is simply learning the association of the 'click' and treat routine. Spend some time practising the 'click and treat' exercise with your dog.

Rapid learning

Being a bright breed, Cavaliers quickly learn that a 'click' means that a treat is coming and you will see your dog recognize this in his behaviour. His ears will prick at the 'click' sound, he may get excited, and his mode of behaviour will show when he expects a treat following the 'click'. Try it and see for yourself.

Clicker training rules

- Always give your dog a treat after a click – even if you have clicked accidentally. He must believe in the 'click means treat' routine.
- Never click the clicker idly or let a child play with it in the dog's hearing. This will confuse him greatly and he will be expecting a tasty treat!
- Only click ONCE. Don't over-react when your dog obeys and produce a constant series of clicks. One click is sufficient.
- You can use the clicker for all the training exercises listed above, simply remembering to click the clicker before rewarding the dog with a treat for carrying out your commands.

Travelling

Teaching your Cavalier how to behave when travelling is also a necessary part of responsible ownership – and it makes for less stressful journeys, too!

Car travel

Dogs, like us humans, can suffer from travel sickness due to the rolling motion of cars, so it is a good idea to get your puppy accustomed to travelling in the car from an early age.

1 Sit with him in a car for a few minutes a day whilst it is stationary to get him used to the environment and smell.
2 Next, turn the engine on, so that your puppy gets used to the noise.
3 Drive around for a short trip in order to familiarize him with the motion of the car. If he is sick, don't scold him – simply clean him up and try again. You may find it useful to have a

second person in the car with you to either do the driving or hold the dog. Don't worry – in time, your Cavalier will become a veteran car traveller.

Car safety

When your Cavalier is older, the safest thing for both of you is to install a dog guard in the back of the car, behind which he will sit in the storage area. Investing in a metal dog crate to fit into the back of a car is also a wise move – again, get him used to being shut in the crate in the same way as if he sleeps in one in the house (see page 34). If your car is too small for a crate or a dog guard, you can buy 'dog seat belts'; these special canine harness restraint straps can

A dog crate is useful for when your Cavalier is travelling in a car. Not only will it keep him safe, but it will also be a snug den for him.

be fitted easily to most cars. Make sure you get the right size for your Cavalier.

A word of warning: cars get hot, especially on sunny days, so never leave your dog unattended in a hot car. It only takes a few minutes for the temperature to rise, and every summer many fatalities occur like this. If you do have to leave your dog in the car for a period of time, always make sure you park in the shade, leave a window or two slightly open to give him fresh air and to keep cool, and water to drink.

You can purchase heat-reflective blankets, which can be placed over his crate, but even so, he should not be left unattended for more than a few minutes.

Public transport

Getting your Cavalier used to public transport is not much different to training him to walk along busy streets. Start him whilst he's a puppy – carry him onto a train, bus or tram (expect to have to pay a fare for him, as most forms of public transport charge for dogs, except for assistance dogs). By all means, let other passengers stroke him and make a fuss of him – it's all good socialization. Don't go on a very long journey to start with – just far enough to get him used to the motion of the vehicle.

A top tip is to take some kitchen paper and plastic bags with you, just in case he has an accident from either end! Remember, too, that animals are rarely allowed on seats, although holding him on your lap should be acceptable. As he grows older, he will get used to travelling and will most likely be quite content to

sit on the floor, preferably under your seat or in front of you – he should not sit in the aisle where he can block other passengers and may get trodden on.

Taking training further

Once your Cavalier is trained to your satisfaction and has learned the basic commands – or even if he is still learning – you may wish to take his training further or to a more formal level. One good way of doing this is to sign up for dog training classes in your area. Ask in your veterinary surgery or check with the local breed club or on the Kennel Club website. Many private dog trainers and dog clubs operate obedience training classes, or you can opt for 'Ringcraft' classes, which not only teach obedience but also the mechanics of dog showing.

Even small breeds, such as Cavaliers, can take part in Agility or Heelwork to Music. So the sky's the limit – it all depends on how much time and effort you want to put in and how co-operative your dog is. Many Cavaliers enjoy competing in all of the above disciplines.

Good Citizens

Several dog training clubs operate the Kennel Club's Good Citizen Test, where dogs (and their owners) have to pass a series of tests to win a certificate – either in Bronze, Silver or Gold categories, growing progressively more advanced.

At its most basic level, the Bronze Award aims to produce a dog that will walk and behave in a controlled manner on the lead, stay in one position on

command and allow his owner to clean, groom and inspect him. The dog does not have to be registered with the Kennel Club and there is no age limit.

The exercises

Dogs are tested in groups and examiners will either award a 'pass' or they will say that the dog is 'not ready'. A pass earns a certificate and, possibly, a rosette.

The scheme is run at many clubs and it is great fun to take part in. The dog has to complete a series of exercises, and the owner is questioned about their responsibility and caring for a dog. The exercises for the Bronze Certificate of the scheme include the following:
• Cleanliness and identification
• Collar and lead

Children can help to train their dog and get involved in the Kennel Club's Good Citizens Test where they can win medals.

• Walking on the lead
• Control at the door
• Controlled walk among people
• Staying for one minute
• Grooming
• Presenting for examination.

Advantages all round

The obvious advantages of group dog training are that you get to meet other dog owners and their dogs and this all helps to better socialize your Cavalier. It is also a wonderful opportunity to make new friends with similar interests as well as being an enjoyable social occasion for all concerned.

Chapter 5

Showing your Cavalier

You probably decided whether to show your Cavalier before you even purchased him. Although no breeder will guarantee that their puppy is going to turn out to be a show champion, they will be reasonably confident as to which puppy best conforms to the Kennel Club Breed Standard (see page 18) and which ones are more 'pet quality'. Having said that, even if you acquired your Cavalier as a family pet, this does not mean that showing him is ruled out, although it would be foolish to expect him to win big prizes and compete at Crufts.

Showing dogs can be fun and an absorbing hobby for people of all ages. You can show your dog in conformation, where he is judged on his looks, or you can show him in obedience and agility, where your training and control will be scrutinized.

Most dog shows are conformation shows. Each breed has a written breed standard, which describes the way a dog of that particular breed should look. Breed standards are usually very specific when it comes to the dog's size, weight, colour, coat and body shape, etc., and the Cavalier's standard is no exception.

Getting started

To be able to take part in most Kennel Club licensed shows, your dog must be at least six months old and KC registered in your name. This procedure should be carried out immediately after you purchase your Cavalier from his breeder (see page 27).

For formal conformation shows, both you and your dog will need to learn show handling. All show dogs must be able to stand still to be assessed by the judge, and to run nicely around the ring. This is not as easy as it seems, and it can take a lot of practice. Different breeds are also handled in different ways. Ask your dog's breeder for advice, and try to find a local dog training club or canine society that has Ringcraft classes; these are invaluable for learning how to handle your dog at shows (see page 82).

Once you have acquired the necessary basic skills to 'show' your Cavalier correctly, you can consider which show

Opposite: Your pet Cavalier could become a show winner like this dog – but it takes a lot of hard work and practice for both you, the owner, and your dog. Most people who start showing dogs soon become hooked.

This Cavalier is standing correctly in a 'free stand' at a show, whilst the judge appraises him. You can learn about how to show your dog to best advantage at ringcraft classes.

you want to enter. There are literally hundreds of dog shows held throughout the year, usually at weekends, and details of these are advertised in the canine newspapers, *Our Dogs* and *Dog World*, as well as online. They are staged by the various dog clubs, which may be specific breed clubs or canine societies. It's a good idea to find and join at least one Cavalier club, which will most likely stage its own show or shows, and it is here that you can gain invaluable advice from your fellow Cavalier enthusiasts (or fanciers as they are often known).

What kind of show?

There are four main types of dog shows: these are Companion, Limit, Open and Championship Shows.

Companion Shows

A good place to start can be the Companion Shows, which are entered on the day and excellent for canine interaction. As well as pedigree classes, they include classes for dogs belonging to the club, fun classes, and handling events where it will be you who is being judged. For details, check out the local and canine press and the Kennel Club website. These shows are often held to raise money for charity, so they have an additional feel good factor.

Limit Shows

These are smaller, less competitive shows, which are good to attend in order to gain experience and knowledge before competing in larger shows. Entry is limited to dogs that have not won certain grades of award and, as such, they are ideal shows for novices to enter.

Open Shows

These are usually inexpensive and local, and are probably the next best place to go after gaining confidence at the smaller Limit Shows. Open Shows usually include all breeds, a breed group or, occasionally, just one single breed.

Championship Shows

The next level up is Championship Shows. These may be held over two to four days, and, again, may be for all breeds, certain breeds or just one. Often they are staged at large venues, such as racecourses and agricultural centres, where the dogs have to be benched when not in the judging ring rather than walked around all day.

The entry to such shows is large with the popular breeds often having entries of over 100 dogs. Your Cavalier can compete at a Championship Show for a Challenge Certificate (CC). If he is fortunate enough to win three CCs from three different judges, he will be classed as a Show Champion (hence Championship Show). Championship Shows are the most expensive, but don't be daunted by this. One of the things you have to learn about dog showing is that you will never get rich from it.

Crufts Dog Show is the world's largest and best-known canine show and is staged by the British Kennel Club. You may have seen coverage of this enormous four-day extravaganza on TV. Here, over 20,000 dogs of all breeds from all over the world compete for the coveted Best of Breed and Group titles, as well as the overall Best In Show. All the dogs entered at Crufts will have had to qualify for entry by winning top placings in the accepted classes at Championship Shows.

Each breed falls into a certain category, namely: Working, Utility, Terrier, Gundog, Hound, Toy, Pastoral, Rare Breeds and Imported Register. Cavaliers fall into the Toy category.

Entering a show

To enter a show you will need to obtain a Show Schedule, which details all the classes and the cost of the entries. Some clubs that operate Ringcraft will have a number of schedules for forthcoming shows, and these can be picked up in person. The schedule will also contain the necessary entry form. If you are sending for a schedule by post, you are advised to send a stamped addressed envelope to the Show Secretary.

Alternatively, many clubs now advertise their shows online and you can download the schedule and entry form. Some really enterprising clubs even take entries online, although most will ask you to send the entry form by post, again enclosing an SAE for the necessary exhibitor's paperwork to be sent back to you.

Useful points

- Some shows have rosettes as well as cards and maybe even trophies, which have been sponsored or donated by individuals or organizations, to be awarded to the winning exhibit of certain classes. The cups and trophies can be engraved with the winner's details and kept for one year.

- Most non-championship show classes are for dogs and bitches together, although in the more popular breeds, classes may be split with the dogs being shown first.

- Companion Shows, Limit Shows, Open Shows and Championship Shows are all held under Kennel Club rules and regulations, which are always printed on the entry schedule. When completing the entry schedule form, take your time, as any mistakes made at this point cannot be rectified on the day of the show when the catalogue has already been printed. If in doubt, ask an experienced exhibitor for help, or contact the Show Secretary who should be only too pleased to advise a novice exhibitor. However, don't leave it until a couple of days before the closing date. Show Secretaries are volunteers and they have lives to lead outside of dog showing, so try to be helpful in return and remember to contact them at a reasonable time of day.

The entry form must be filled in with your Cavalier's details, including details of his parents (which can be found on his pedigree) as well as the breeder's name and your own name, address and telephone number. This must be sent off with the entry fee by a set date before the actual show date. The form will have a closing date on it and any entries received after that date will not be allowed. Once the Show Secretary has received the entries, a catalogue of all the dogs entered is compiled and made available to everyone on the show day.

Which class?

The shows are based on classes and the winner of each class goes through to a final to become Best In Show. The usual classes offered include: Minor Puppy, Puppy, Junior, Special Yearling, Maiden, Novice, Undergraduate, Graduate, Post Graduate, Limit and Open, and possibly Veteran. In many multi-breed shows, the winners of each Breed class will compete in the Group class – so Cavaliers will be competing for Best Toy. The winners of each Group then compete for Best In Show. This is known as judging on the 'group system.'

Your dog will have to meet certain conditions before he can be entered into a class, based on his previous show experience. Obviously, an Adult Dog cannot compete in the Puppy class, whilst an experienced show dog would not be entered in the Novice class if he has won at previous shows. You may enter your dog in more than one class at the show. The number of placings per

This owner takes her dogs to the show ring in a special wheeled crate, which doubles as a grooming table. This is a useful piece of equipment if you plan to show your dog.

class – i.e. 1st, 2nd, 3rd, Reserve, etc. – is decided by the show committee and thus varies from show to show.

Preparations

If the show is a larger one, such as a Championship Show, the Show Secretary will post you your exhibitor's number – the number that applies to your Cavalier in the catalogue – together with a car park pass, if one is on offer, and any additional information about the show.

If you are disabled, make sure that you state this on the entry form – some societies request a photocopy of your blue badge in order o ensure that you get easy parking.

Exhibit number

One small but essential, and often overlooked, piece of show equipment is the number, dog clip or arm band holder. You will need to display your dog's exhibit number somewhere on your person. True, you could use a safety pin, but most exhibitors opt for a small pin-on clip, which holds the card in its 'jaws'. Nice and light to wear, it makes the exhibit number easy to see for the judge and stewards and is well worth buying if you attend many shows.

Your own bag

Finally, pack a bag for you. Sometimes dog shows can drag on quite a bit and, although refreshments are usually available at most shows, you might not like what's on offer – or the prices – so take a packed lunch and something to drink with you. A change of shoes or some other clothing might also be a good idea, especially if it rains. It may sound obvious, but take some extra money, too – quite often there are trade stands at shows and you might just see that particular item that you have been seeking for your Cavalier for ages, and you'll want to buy it.

Equipment

You would be well advised to invest in a transporting cage. This wheeled crate will keep your Cavalier safe and free from mud on the way into the show. As many shows are held outdoors, the last thing you need is a well-groomed show dog getting dirty. Some transport pens even fold down into grooming tables once you have benched your dog. If not, a grooming table is another essential item of equipment. These can be purchased at shows or through advertisements in specialist canine publications (you might even see a good second-hand one advertised on Ebay). If you are bringing your own fold-down table as a grooming table, make sure you pack your rubber car mat or the piece of carpet you normally use when grooming, so your dog will not slip on (or off) the table.

You will also need to pack a show bag for your dog. This should contain his dog coat if the show is held on a cold wet day or a heat-reflective one for hot days at outside shows, together with all the grooming and show equipment you need, including:

- Brushes, combs and grooming mitt
- Eye cleanser
- Grooming powder or lotion/spray – remember that it is against the rules if a judge finds powder in a dog's coat, so always brush it out beforehand
- Claw clippers
- Nail file
- Show lead: a lighter, usually slip-on, lead for guiding your dog correctly in the show ring
- Some small treats – liver or cheese pieces are ideal – to pop in your pocket and use to gain your dog's attention in the ring
- A small amount of dog food if you think your Cavalier will need it (although many exhibitors never feed their dogs at shows)
- Water bowl and a bottle of water. Of course, you can get water from the taps in toilets at show venues, but it's a safeguard to bring along some local water that your Cavalier is used to drinking. Dogs are very sensitive to differences in water taste out of their usual area.

Grooming

Needless to say, you will have bathed and groomed your Cavalier before the show and made sure that his coat is in good condition and looking its best. Your dog's breeder is probably the best person to consult for grooming tips as they will be as keen as you for the dog to look good in the show ring.

You need to groom yourself, too. Dog shows can be fun, but no-one exhibits their pristine show dogs whilst they themselves are dressed in grubby old jeans and trainers. It would be a great shame to have an immaculately presented Cavalier on show, only for him to be let down by the scruffy person at the end of his lead.

Appearances do count at dog shows – and this applies to the exhibitor as well as the dog, so make an effort.

Dress smartly, but comfortably; you are going to have to be walking and trotting round the show ring with your dog, so you need to wear something that not only looks good but also gives you plenty of freedom of movement. Above all, wear sensible shoes.

The day of the show

When the big day dawns, no matter how you are travelling to the show, give yourself plenty of time for the journey and to get your Cavalier benched,

This well groomed Cavalier has been well prepared by his owner for the show.

groomed and settled when you arrive at the show. Be prepared for an early start (and possibly a late finish). It is a good idea to have more than one person in your 'show team', as you will need help with plenty of tasks. Besides which, you may want to look around the show and although you can leave your dog in his crate or bench, you still need to be safety minded. The general public often wander around the benches at shows and want to pat the dogs. Even if your dog is the friendliest Cavalier who ever lived, he will still get nervous if a stranger approaches him whilst he is on his own in a strange environment, so make sure that one person stays at the bench with the dog at all times.

Into the ring

When the moment arrives for your class to be judged, you will both file into the ring to take your place in the line up. Give you and your dog plenty of space between the dogs and exhibitors to either side of you. Stand your dog in the appropriate show stance – although Cavaliers are classed as a 'free standing' breed – to get him used to the fact that it's 'game on' time. Again, holding up a treat can help to keep his attention focused on you. The steward will check your exhibit number to confirm your attendance and then it's time for the judge to take over.

The judging process

The judge will usually 'walk the ring' once, taking a general look at all the exhibits. Make sure your dog is in the correct show stance and paying attention. Each exhibit is then judged individually, with the owner and dog moving up the line as they are judged. You will place your Cavalier on the judging table, again ensuring a good stance ready for when the judge inspects him, carefully checking his body, legs, tail, head, ears, eyes and teeth – none of which your Cavalier should object to. Don't speak to the judge unless you are

---

Show tips

- When you have groomed and primped your Cavalier to your satisfaction, you may want to watch the various classes being judged before its your turn. Study the catalogue to see who your dog is up against.
- Make sure you are at the appropriate judging ring (the area where judging takes place) in good time before your class.
- Keep your Cavalier focused on you and don't allow him to get distracted by all the other dogs and people milling around.
- If he has been well trained at Ringcraft, he will probably be quite patient, but giving him plenty of encouragement (and a treat or two) will better guarantee his attention.
- Arriving in good time may offer the chance of a little practice in a ring before your class starts at Open Shows.

spoken to, and only speak to your dog if it is necessary to gain his attention, reassure him or to follow commands.

After the first inspection, the judge will ask you to put your dog on the ground and walk in either a triangle or a straight line, returning to him at the end of it. This is where all that Ringcraft training should pay off: your Cavalier should execute the perfect show walk and turn immaculately with you to come back to the judge where you will stand him again. The judge will take one more look at him and then ask you to move to the back of the line behind the other dogs that have been judged.

You can both relax a bit more now whilst the other dogs are being judged. There's nothing wrong with chatting quietly to other exhibitors, but only do

so if it is appropriate. The key thing to remember is that you are all in competition against each other and want your own dogs to win, so, ideally, concentrate on your dog rather than your competitors.

Once the judge has judged each exhibit, he will usually walk the ring again, so stand your Cavalier correctly and wait until he has concluded his deliberations. The time has come to choose the best exhibits. Sometimes, in large classes the judge will require you all to walk the ring again together, and he may make a 'cut', calling out a number of dogs in no particular order and asking the other exhibitors and their dogs to leave the ring. He will look over the remaining dogs again, or ask you to walk for him again. Finally, he will call out the winners in order.

If you are very lucky, you will be pronounced the winner, in which case you will be needed again when all the Cavalier classes are finished for Best of Breed, Reserve Best of Breed and Best Puppy in Breed (sex at Championship Shows).

If you don't get a first place but get awarded something else, consider how many other dogs in total were entered in the class – to be placed in a big class

The judge will carefully inspect your dog's coat, muscle and bone structure as well as the shape of his body and head.

is an achievement in itself. Above all, be gracious in victory and defeat – most fanciers are good sports and they will congratulate and applaud the winner.

If you don't get placed, however, don't be downhearted – there's always the next time. After the show you could ask the judge where you went wrong and they should be pleased to tell you when they have time to chat. Don't be offended if the judge has to leave or is busy with other breeds. Listen to what you are told and then learn from it for the next time.

Fun shows

If your Cavalier has no papers or is 'pet' quality, you can still show him at a Companion Show, which is KC licensed and run within the limits of KC rules.

This owner is holding her Cavalier correctly so that the judge can appraise him. You will need to get your dog accustomed to being handled by people he does not know.

These are fun shows, which are mostly held to raise money for good causes, and all dogs over six months of age are welcome – with the exception of top show winners, such as CC winners and Champions. No papers are needed, but many people start their dog's show career here, and others come along to support and enjoy a more relaxed experience than at the other shows.

There will be pedigree classes, but not one for each breed – rather one per group of dogs, e.g. one for all sporting breeds (terriers, gundogs, etc.) and one for all non-sporting breeds (toy dogs, working and pastoral breeds, etc.). There may also be classes for the Best Crossbreed and others just for fun, along the lines of 'Dog With The Waggiest Tail' or 'Dog Most Like Its Owner'. There also have to be a few classes for those dogs who are members of the Companion Dog Club – it's the dog who belongs, not you! These shows are normally held outdoors in summer or in venues such as church halls at any time of the year, and they are great fun for dogs and their owners alike – a good place to start your Cavalier's show career. Entries are made on the day and the entry fees are minimal.

Postscript

Whichever show you exhibit at and whatever placing your Cavalier gets, you always take the best dog home at the end of the day – your dog! Enjoy showing and it will enrich both your lives.

This judge is studying the dog's gait as the owner walks him up and down the show ring.

PART TWO

HEALTHCARE

As a good owner, it is your responsibility to keep your Cavalier King Charles Spaniel fit and healthy. If you follow the basic guidelines in this book and socialize him, feed a nutritious diet, exercise him adequately, groom and play with him, you can prevent many common health problems. However, it is important that you learn to recognize the warning signs of problems and diseases so that you can treat them yourself or seek professional help from your vet before they get worse. Prevention is always preferable to cure, and a healthy, contented dog will become your trusted companion for many years.

Signs of good health

Anal region This should be clean without any faeces clinging to the fur. The dog should not lick this area excessively or drag his rear along the ground.

Body The dog's body should be firm and well-muscled. He should not carry excess weight nor be so thin that his ribs stick out.

Ears They should be responsive to any sound. The insides should be pale pink with no visible wax or unpleasant smell. Your dog should not shake his head or scratch his ears too often.

Eyes The eyes should be bright, alert and without any signs of discharge, swelling or tear stains. A tiny amount of 'sleep' in the inner corners is quite normal.

Nose The nose of a healthy dog should be cold and damp without any discharge. Occasionally, there may be a little clear fluid.

Teeth Healthy teeth are white and smooth, not yellow, which is a sign of plaque and tartar formation. The breath should not smell unpleasant and there should be no loose or missing teeth or inflamed or bleeding gums.

Coat The coat should be in good condition and should smell pleasantly 'doggy'. It should be glossy and pleasant to touch. When you part the hairs, there should be no signs of fleas' droppings, sore or bare patches.

Claws The claws should end level with the pad and not be too long. Look out for broken claws, damage to dew claws (if they have not been removed) and hay seeds embedded in the pads.

Hereditary diseases

As in humans, dogs can inherit a wide range of diseases, and some of these may occur in Cavalier King Charles Spaniels. They are caused by genetic faults or aberrations in the breeding line.

Genetic faults

The genetic background to many hereditary ailments can be extremely complicated and is of concern to all professional breeders, veterinarians and geneticists. Screening tests are available for tendencies to some hereditary diseases, and potential owners of dogs, particularly pedigrees, should consult their vet about possible inherited health problems within the breed and ask the breeder about the lineage and history of the dams and sires before purchasing a puppy. Although some hereditary diseases are treatable, the underlying genetic faults cannot be eliminated.

Hip dysplasia

One of the most common inherited diseases, this affects a significant number of Cavalier King Charles Spaniels. In a normal, healthy dog, the hip is a 'ball and socket' joint, allowing a wide range of movement. The rounded end at the top of the femur fits tightly into the cup-shaped socket in the pelvis. In hip dysplasia, a shallow socket develops with a distorted femur head and slack joint ligaments. There can be excessive movement between the femur and pelvis, leading to a malfunctioning joint which will gradually become arthritic.

Early symptoms

If a puppy develops severe hip dysplasia he may have difficulty in walking. Getting up from a sitting position may be painful and he will cry out. When he runs, he may use both hind legs together in a 'bunny hop' or may look as though he is swaying.

These tell-tale symptoms may be identifiable from five months onwards. Mildly affected puppies may show no signs at all of hip dysplasia at this age, but they will begin to develop arthritis (see page 115) at approximately eight years of age.

Hip dysplasia scheme

The British Veterinary Association and the Kennel Club run a joint scheme (the BVA/KC hip dysplasia scheme) based on hip scoring. The vet submits the X-ray, bearing the KC registration number of the dog, to the scheme. Each hip is then scored from 0 to 54, making a total of 108 maximum between the two hips. The lower the score the better, and 0:0 is the best score possible.

You should not breed from a dog or bitch with a higher hip score than the average for the breed or hip dysplasia will never be reduced or eliminated from that breed.

When buying a puppy, check that both the parents have been X-rayed, scored, and have achieved a low score. This does not guarantee that the puppy will not develop hip dysplasia but it does reduce the chances of it happening.

Treatment

If mild hip dysplasia is treated in a growing puppy by anabolic steroids, limiting exercise and diet, he will often grow into a healthy adult dog. However, you may have to restrict his exercise later on in life, too. In severe cases, surgery is available.

Syringomyelia

This is a condition that is caused by developmental malformation of occipital bones in the skull which puts pressure on the spinal cord and the consequent formation of fluid-filled cavities in the latter. The symptoms include neck pain and over-sensitivity to touch, persistent scratching at the head, neck or nothing in particular, especially when on the lead and screaming for no apparent reason. Some experts believe that 50 per cent of Cavalier King Charles Spaniels have the abnormality, although only a much smaller proportion are affected severely enough to show clinical signs. Diagnosis involves radiography or, best, MRI scanning, and treatment is by surgery and medication.

Other hereditary conditions

Cavalier King Charles Spaniels are more prone than some other breeds to the following ailments listed below.

Chronic mitral valve disease

This heart condition is an inherited disease of Cavaliers. The symptoms include fainting episodes, weakness and breathlessness. Diagnosis is by stethoscope auscultation, X-ray and echocardiogram. All Cavaliers should be auscultated by a vet when they are one year old and once a year thereafter. Medical treatment can relieve the condition.

Eye problems

Around 40 per cent of all Cavaliers have some form of eye problem. They include the following conditions.

Cataract

A hardening and opacity of the lens of the eye, cataract can be hereditary and is seen in young Cavaliers, or is the result in later life of diabetes or old age degeneration. Treatment is by surgical removal of the lens.

Retinal Dysplasia

This malformation of the retina of the eye causes deficient vision, which can vary from not being noticeable by the owner to complete blindness. Diagnosis is by veterinary ophthalmoscopy. There is no cure.

Corneal dystrophy of the eye

This is the development of greyish deposits of fat and calcium within the corneas of both eyes, usually between two and four years of age. Vision is not affected and treatment is unnecessary.

Entropion and distichiasis

In entropion, the edge of the eyelid folds inward, while distichiasis is the existence of abnormally positioned eyelashes, which rub against the eyeball. With both these conditions, eye irritation and inflammation result. They can be surgically corrected.

Keratoconjunctivitis sicca

This inflammation of the eye surfaces is due to deficiency of tear lubrication, and although it can be relieved by veterinary medication it cannot be cured.

Epilepsy

This can occur in Cavaliers and is the occurrence of seizures that can vary in degree and duration. Diagnosis may involve using electro-encephalography or even CT or MRI scans. Epilepsy can be controlled by veterinary medication.

Patella luxation

This condition is dislocation of the kneecap. The kneecap may slip back into place automatically or may need a vet to facilitate it, but repeated luxation requires surgical correction to prevent osteoarthritis developing later.

Episodic Falling Syndrome

This disease of Cavaliers is unique to the breed. Symptoms vary and include sudden rigidity of muscles, loss of coordination and collapse. It can be confused with other conditions, such as epilepsy or syringomyelia. There are no diagnostic tests available. Treatment by medication, particularly by clonazepam, is effective.

'Fly biting'

Sometimes called 'Flycatcher's' syndrome, this condition of snapping at imaginary flies can begin as early as eight months of age and may be a symptom of syringomyelia, a form of partial epileptic seizure or a compulsive disorder. There is no specific test for the condition but owners should seek the advice of a veterinary neurologist. Treatment may be by anti-convulsant medication or via an animal behaviourist.

Note: All these conditions require veterinary attention as soon as they appear.

Preventing disease

Prevention is always better than cure and there is a lot you can do to prevent health problems developing by keeping your dog in first-class condition. Get into the habit of inspecting his ears, eyes, teeth, coat, paws and rear end.

Check your dog

Groom your dog on a regular basis. These sessions are a good opportunity to examine your dog.

1 Look inside his mouth, checking that his teeth are clean and white and his breath does not smell unpleasant. Clean the teeth with special toothpaste at least once a week.
2 Next check his eyes, nose and ears for signs of any discharge, odour or inflammation. Keep them clean by wiping them gently with some damp cotton wool.
3 Examine the dog's coat, looking for

bald patches, excessive hair loss, tell-tale signs of fleas (black sooty specks in the fur) and soiling around the anus and rear end. The coat should look healthy and glossy, and the dog should not scratch excessively.

4 Pick up each of his paws and check the pads and claws, which should not be broken nor too long. If your dog appears to be limping, look for cuts or any swellings on the pads. Some dog breeds are susceptible to grass and hay seeds becoming embedded in their pads.

Note: If you find anything unusual or suspect there may be a health problem, then make an appointment to take your dog to the vet. Even if it is only a minor worry, this will set your mind at rest. You can treat the problem before it gets more serious and learn how to prevent it recurring in the future.

Diet is important

Feeding a balanced, nutritious diet will help to keep your dog healthy. It is important not to over-feed him or he may gain too much weight and this can lead to many health problems that are associated with obesity as well as a reduced life expectancy. Diabetes, heart problems and difficulty in coping with arthritic conditions occur more frequently in overweight dogs.

Adult Cavaliers should weigh 5.4–8.2kg (12–18lb). The end of the rib cage should be detectable visually with no fatty expansion of the loins or pot belly. If you give your dog proprietary foods, follow the maker's directions but, if you are unsure as to which foods to

offer, how much and how often to feed your dog, ask your vet for advice. Similarly, if your dog loses his appetite or sheds weight suddenly, consult your vet – the dog may well need worming (see page 106) or the symptoms may be a sign of a more serious problem. Your vet can also advise on a slimming regime for your overweight dog and may run canine slimming classes.

Keep your dog fit

All dogs need regular exercise every day to keep fit and stay in optimum health. The amount and type, however, will vary according to the breed. Thus a toy breed, such as the Cavalier King Charles, can be adequately exercised by a stroll round the garden and a walk round the block each day, plus games in the garden.

Stimulate your dog

Playing games with your dog and teaching him tricks will provide both mental and physical stimulation. Lively dogs like Cavaliers need to be busy and active, or they soon become bored and this can lead to behaviour problems as well as to poor health.

Vaccinations

The most important thing you can do to protect your dog's health is to make sure that he is vaccinated against the major infectious canine diseases. These are distemper, infectious canine hepatitis, 'kennel cough', parvovirus and the two forms of leptospirosis. Vaccination against all these serious ailments can be given by your vet in one shot when a puppy is at least six weeks of age.

A second dose is administered three to six weeks later. An annual booster dose is recommended thereafter to top up your dog's immunity, although some veterinary authorities believe this is not necessary. However, like most vets, I personally am in favour of it.

In addition, in some countries, the vaccination of dogs against rabies is obligatory. Puppies can be vaccinated as early as four weeks of age. Yearly booster shots are essential.

Pet Passports

If you are considering taking your dog on holiday to one of the European Union countries or to certain other designated rabies-free countries, you must obtain a Pet Passport. The same applies to dogs travelling abroad to dog shows and competitive events. Your vet and the local DEFRA office will give you information on how to go about this. The dog will have to be micro-chipped, vaccinated against rabies and blood tested 30 days after vaccination before you leave for your trip, and then treated against ticks and other parasites 24 to 48 hours before your return with a veterinary certificate to prove it. You must have a DEFRA PETS re-entry certificate certifying that the blood test gave a positive result for immunity against rabies after the vaccination, and you will have to sign a declaration that the dog did not leave the qualifying countries while you were away.

Neutering

Unless you are definitely contemplating breeding from your dog, it is best, for the dog and for you, to have a bitch spayed or a dog castrated after they reach six months of age. Castration reduces aggressiveness and the likelihood of a dog going a-roaming. Spaying, apart from avoiding the arrival of unwanted puppies, reduces the chances of breast tumours in later life and, obviously, the onset of common uterine disease, such as pyometra. Neither castration nor spaying change the character of dogs nor necessarily make them put on weight. Talk to your vet about what is involved.

Parasites

External parasites

These parasites live on the surface of the dog's body, and include lice, fleas, ticks, mites (see page 116) and ringworm (see page 117). Keep a look out for them and treat an infected dog as quickly as possible.

Fleas

Dogs are usually infested by their own species of flea – and the cat's – but sometimes they can carry rabbit, human or hedgehog fleas. The infestations are more likely to be worse in warm weather in the summer, but fleas thrive all the year round, particularly if your home has central heating. Sometimes it is extremely difficult to find any fleas on a dog, but just a single flea can cause an allergic reaction when piercing a dog's skin and injecting its saliva.

Such a reaction can result in widespread irritation, skin sores and rashes. Flea eggs do not stick to the dog's hair like those of lice (see below), but, being dry, they drop off onto carpets and furniture.

> **COMMON SYMPTOMS**
> • **An affected dog will keep scratching**
> • **Tiny reddish scabs or papules appear on the skin, particularly on the dog's back**
> • **Flea droppings look like coal dust in the coat.**

What you can do Use insecticidal sprays, shampoos or powders, which are obtainable from the vet, chemist or a pet shop, at regular intervals throughout the summer. Treat the floors, furniture and your pet's favourite sleeping places, basket and bedding with a specially formulated aerosol product every seven months. This procedure effectively stops the re-infestation of dogs by larvae emerging from eggs in the environment.

Lice

There are two kinds: biting lice which feed on skin scales; and sucking lice which draw tissue fluids from the skin. The latter cause more irritation to the dog than the former. Lice are greyish-white and about 2mm (⅛in) in length. Their eggs (nits) are white and cemented to the dog's hairs. The dog louse does not fancy humans or cats and will not infest them.

> **COMMON SYMPTOMS**
> • **The dog will scratch himself**
> • **Lice and nits will be visible to the naked eye when the dog's coat is carefully searched.**

What you can do Sprays, powders or baths are available from the vet or pet shop. Apply on at least three occasions at five- to seven-day intervals to kill adults and the larvae that hatch from the nits.

Ticks

More often seen on country dogs than town dogs, ticks suck blood, their abdomen swelling up as they do so. The commonest tick of dogs is the sheep tick. It clings to the dog's hair, generally on the legs, head or under-belly, and pierces the skin with its mouth parts. In doing so it can transmit an organism called Borrelia, a cause of Lyme Disease. Characterized by lameness and heart disease, it requires veterinary diagnosis by means of blood tests, and then treatment using specific antibiotics and anti-inflammatory drugs.

What you can do Remove a tick by dabbing it with some alcohol, such as gin or methylated spirits, and then wait a few minutes for its head to relax before grasping it near to the mouthparts with fine tweezers – you can buy special ones for this job. You can dislodge the tick with a little jerk. Do not ever pull it off without applying the alcohol first as the mouthparts left in the skin may cause an abscess to form.

An alternative method is to spray the tick with some flea spray and then to remove it the following day. The regular application of a flea spray or fitting your dog with an insecticidal collar during the summer months is highly recommended in order to control tick infestation effectively.

Internal parasites

These parasites live inside the dog's body. Several kinds of worm can infest dogs and, in very rare cases, these parasites can spread to human beings.

Roundworms

These live, when adult, in the dog's intestines but their immature forms migrate through their host's body, damaging such organs as the liver and lungs, particularly those of puppies.

Hookworms and whipworms

These blood-sucking parasites can cause severe anaemia. Your vet will be able to confirm if your dog is affected.

Tapeworms and roundworms

The commonest dog tapeworm, *Dipylidium*, is spread by fleas, in which its larvae develop. You can see the segments of this tapeworm looking like wriggling white grains of rice in droppings or stuck to the hair around the dog's bottom. Roundworms cause the most trouble for dogs, particularly puppies.

COMMON SYMPTOMS
- Symptoms of roundworms include bowel upsets, emaciation, fits, chest and liver malfunction
- Tapeworms may cause dogs to drag their rear ends ('scoot') along the floor.

What you can do To treat roundworms you should give your dog a 'worming' medication which will be available from your vet. Puppies usually should receive their first dose at three weeks of age. Repeat the worming every three weeks until they are 16 weeks old, repeating at six months and twice a year thereafter.

Give your dog anti-tapeworm medication once a year or when any worm segments are seen in his droppings or on the hair near and around the anus. Regular flea control will also help you to combat tapeworms. Some worm treatments are effective against all types of internal parasites, and you should consult your veterinary surgeon about which products are suitable and the correct dosage.

Dental care

Check your dog's teeth regularly and brush them once or twice a week to prevent any tartar building up. Gnawing on a variety of bones and chews will help to keep his teeth clean and healthy.

Tooth disease

It is relatively easy to spot the common symptoms of tooth disease and dental decay (see right).

COMMON SYMPTOMS
- Your dog may salivate (slavering) at the mouth
- He may paw at his mouth
- His chewing motions may be exaggerated
- He may chew tentatively as if he is dealing with a hot potato
- His breath may smell unpleasant.

What you can do Cleaning the dog's teeth once or twice weekly with cotton wool or a soft toothbrush (you can buy special ones for dogs) which has been dipped in salt water (or some specially formulated dog toothpaste) will stop tartar formation. 'Bones' and 'chews' made of processed hide (available from good pet shops) and the occasional meal of coarse-cut, raw butcher's meat also help to prevent it building up.

Tartar
When tartar, a yellowy-brown, cement-like substance, accumulates, it does not produce holes in the teeth that need filling. Instead it damages the gum edge, lets in bacteria to infect the tooth sockets and thus loosens the teeth.

Tartar always causes some gum inflammation (gingivitis – see below) and frequently bad breath. If your pet displays the symptoms described, open his mouth and look for a foreign body stuck between his teeth. This may be a sliver of wood or bone stuck between two adjacent molars at the back of the mouth or a bigger object jammed across the upper teeth against the hard palate. You can usually flick out foreign bodies with a teaspoon handle.

Gingivitis
Bright red edging to the gums where they meet the teeth, together with ready bleeding on even gentle pressure, are the principal signs of gingivitis (gum disease). Tap each tooth with your finger or a pencil. If there are any signs of looseness or tenderness, you should wash the dog's mouth with some warm water and salt, and give him an aspirin tablet. There is little else you can do without seeking professional help. Take the dog to the vet and ask his advice.

Broken teeth
Sometimes a dog will break a tooth, perhaps by fighting or chewing stones (a bad habit that some dogs get into). The large 'fang' teeth (the canines) are most often the ones that are damaged. These injuries do not usually produce any signs of toothache, root infection or death of the tooth.

Treatments used in human dentistry, such as fillings, root treatments or crowning, may be necessary and they are all possible nowadays.

Ulcers and tumours
Mouth ulcers, tumours (juvenile warts are common in young dogs) and tonsillitis will all need veterinary diagnosis and treatment where they are the cause of some of the symptoms mentioned above.

Canine dentistry
This is easily tackled by your vet. Using tranquillizers or short-acting general anaesthetics, tartar can be removed from a dog's teeth with scrapers or an ultra-sonic scaling machine. Antibacterial drugs may be prescribed if encroaching tartar has caused secondary gum infection. Bad teeth must be taken out to prevent root abscesses and socket infection from causing problems, such as septicaemia, sinusitis or even kidney disease, elsewhere in the affected dog's body.

Eye problems

Your dog's eyes are precious and you must check regularly that they are normal and healthy. Cavalier King Charles Spaniels are prone to a number of serious eye diseases (see page 101).

(see page 101).

> **COMMON SYMPTOMS**
> • Sore, runny or 'mattery' eyes
> • Blue or white film over the eye
> • Partially or totally closed eye or eyes.

Watering and discharge

If just one of the dog's eyes is involved and the only symptom is watering or a sticky discharge without any marked irritation, you can try washing the eye gently with boracic acid powder in warm water once every few hours, followed by the introduction of a little Golden Eye ointment (which is obtainable from the chemist) onto the affected eyeball. If any symptoms in or around the eyes last for more than a day, you must take the patient to the veterinary clinic and get professional treatment. Particularly in young dogs, two mattery eyes may indicate distemper (see page 110).

Eye conditions

Persistent watering of one or both eyes can be due to a very slight infolding of the eyelid (see opposite), or to blocked tear ducts. A blue or white film over one or both eyes is normally a sign of keratitis, which is an inflammation of the cornea. This is not a cataract but it does require immediate veterinary attention. Opacity of the lens (cataract) can be seen as a blue or white 'film' much deeper in the eye. The pupil looks greyish in colour instead of the usual black. This usually occurs in elderly dogs but it may be seen sometimes in young puppies (congenital cataract) and also at other ages (old age cataract and diabetic cataract).

Inflammations of the eye

Inflammations can be treated by the veterinarian in a variety of ways. Antibiotic injections, drops and ointments are available, plus various other drugs to reduce inflammation, as are surgical methods of tackling ulcerated eyes under local anaesthesia. Problems due to deformed eyelids, foreign bodies embedded in the eyeball and even some cataracts can all be treated surgically nowadays.

Other eye problems

This breed is more prone than many other dogs to the following conditions:
• Cataract
• Retinal dysplasia (folds in the retina)
• Corneal dystrophy
• Keratoconjunctivitis sicca (inflammation of the eye surfaces due to deficiency of tear lubrication).

Note: These eye conditions all require veterinary diagnosis and can, in some cases, be improved when treated but not necessarily cured. If you suspect an eye problem, see your vet.

Ear problems

A healthy dog's ears should be alert and responsive to sounds. The ear flaps of most breeds are usually pale pink and silky inside, and there should be no wax or nasty odour. A dog who keeps scratching his ears and shaking his head may have an ear infection.

COMMON SYMPTOMS
- **Shaking the head and scratching the ear**
- **It is painful when the ear is touched**
- **There may be a bad smell and discharge**
- **The dog tilts his head to one side**
- **There is ballooning of the ear flap.**

Preventing problems

Clean your dog's ears once a week. Cavaliers usually have some hair growing in the ear canal. Pluck out the hair between finger and thumb. Don't cut it. Using 'baby buds' or twists of cotton wool moistened in warm olive oil, clean the ear with a twisting action to remove excess brown ear wax. You should always see the vet early with any ear trouble. Chronic ear complaints can be very difficult to eradicate.

Treating minor problems

If symptoms suddenly appear and the dog is in distress, an effective emergency treatment is to pour a little warmed (not hot) liquid paraffin carefully into the affected ear. Acute inflammation will be greatly soothed by the oil. Don't stuff proprietary liquids into a dog's ear; you do not know what you may be treating. Most of all, avoid those so-called canker powders as the powder bases of these products can cause additional irritation by forming annoying accumulations that act as foreign bodies.

Ear irritation

This may be due to various things that find their way into the ear canal. Grass awns may need professional removal. Small, barely visible white mange mites that live in dog's ears cause itching, and bacteria can set up secondary infections. Sweaty, dirty conditions, particularly in the poorly ventilated ears of breeds like Cavaliers with their long, well 'feathered' ear flaps, provide an ideal opportunity for germs to multiply. The vet will decide whether mites, bacteria, fungi or other causes are the source of inflammation, and will use antiparasitic, antibiotic or antifungal drugs as drops or injections.

Middle-ear disease

Although tilting of the head may be due simply to severe irritation on one side, it can indicate that the middle ear, the deeper part beyond the eardrum, is involved. Middle-ear disease does not necessarily result from outer-ear infection but may arise from trouble in the Eustachian tube which links the middle ear to the throat. This will always require some rigorous veterinary attention with the use of antiflammatory drugs, antibiotics and, more rarely, deep drainage operations.

Nose problems

Don't allow your dog's nostrils ever to get caked and clogged up. Bathe them thoroughly with warm water and anoint the nose pad with some soothing cold cream. If there are any 'common cold' symptoms, you must seek veterinary advice immediately.

> **COMMON SYMPTOMS**
> • The dog's nostrils are running and mattery
> • The dog appears to have the equivalent of a human common cold
> • The nose tip is sore, cracked and dry
> • Check the eyes as well as the nose – if they are both mattery, the dog may have distemper.

Sore noses

Old dogs with cracked, dry nose pads need regular attention to keep their nostrils free and to deal with bleeding from the cracks. Bathe the nose frequently, applying cod liver oil ointment twice or three times daily and working it in well. Your vet may prescribe multivitamins or corticosteroid preparations.

Rhinitis and sinusitis

Sneezing, a mattery discharge from the nostrils, head shaking and, perhaps, nose bleed may indicate rhinitis (the inflammation of the nasal passages) or sinusitis (inflammation within one or more of the sinus chambers in the skull). Bacterial, viral or fungal germs, foreign bodies, growths, tooth abscesses or eye disease can be the cause.

Like humans, dogs possess air-filled spaces in the bones of their skulls (sinuses) which can become diseased. Infections or tumours can occur in these cavities. Sometimes an infection can spread into them from a bad tooth root nearby. The signs of sinusitis include sneezing, persistent nasal discharge and head shaking. If you notice these symptoms, take your dog to the vet.

Respiratory problems

Dogs can suffer from bronchitis, pleurisy, pneumonia, heart disease and

> **COMMON SYMPTOMS**
> • The dog may cough
> • There may be some wheezing and sneezing
> • The dog's breathing may be laboured.

other chest conditions. Coughing and sneezing, the signs of a 'head cold', possibly together with mattery eyes, diarrhoea and listlessness, may indicate distemper – a serious virus disease.

Distemper

Although this is more common in younger animals, it can occur at any age and shows a variety of symptom combinations. Dogs catching distemper can recover although the outlook is serious if there are symptoms such as fits, uncontrollable limb twitching or paralysis, which suggest that the disease has affected the nervous system. These may not appear until many weeks after the virus first invades the body.

What you can do Your dog should be vaccinated against distemper and other important canine viral and leptospiral diseases at the first opportunity – when he is a puppy after reaching six weeks of age – and make sure that you keep the annual booster dose going. At the first signs of any generalized illness, perhaps resembling 'flu' or a 'cold', contact the vet. Keep the dog warm, give him plenty of liquids and provide easily digestible nourishing food.

Treatment
Your vet will be able to confirm whether the dog has distemper. Because it is caused by a virus, the disease is very difficult to treat. Antibiotics and other drugs are used to suppress any dangerous secondary bacterial infections. Vitamin injections will help to strengthen the body's defences. The debilitating effects of coughing, diarrhoea and vomiting are countered by drugs which reduce these symptoms.

Coughs
Where troublesome coughs occur in the older dog, give a half to two codeine tablets three times a day, depending on the animal's size, but see the vet.

Heart disease
This is common in elderly dogs and often responds well to treatment. Under veterinary supervision, drugs can give a new lease of life to dogs with 'dicky' hearts. It is useful in cases of heart trouble and in all older dogs to give vitamin E in the synthetic form (50–200mgm per day depending on the dog's size) or as wheat germ oil capsules (two to six per day).

Cavalier King Charles Spaniels are predisposed to the commonest heart condition of dogs – chronic mitral valve (see page 101). It is probably hereditary and, although primarily affecting middle-aged and older animals, it can begin to produce symptoms at one to three years of age.

Symptoms vary depending on the severity of the condition and include chronic cough,intolerance of exercise and tiring easily, breathing difficulties, build-up of fluid in the abdomen and bouts of fainting. Veterinary diagnosis may involve auscultation to detect heart murmurs, radiography and electrocardiography. Provided congestive heart failure does not develop, medical management can be very successful.

Bronchitis
Inflammation of the tubes that conduct air through the lungs can be caused by a variety of bacteria and viruses, parasitic lungworms, allergy, inhalation of dust, smoke, foreign bodies or excessive barking. Specific therapy is applied by the vet and sometimes, in the case of foreign bodies, surgery or the use of a fibre-optic bronchoscope is necessary.

Pneumonia

There are many causes in dogs, the commonest being infections by micro-organisms such as viruses or bacteria. Migrating parasitic worm larvae and inhalation of foreign bodies are less frequent. The signs are faster and/or more laboured breathing, a cough, raised temperature and, often, nasal discharge. It can be treated with antibiotics, corticosteroids, 'cough' medicines and medication. Pneumonia always demands immediate professional attention.

Kennel cough

This condition is caused by a bacterium (*Bordetella*) or viruses (Canine parainfluenza virus, Canine herpes virus or Canine adenovirus) or a mixture of these. The signs are a dry cough, often with sneezing, and a moderate eye and nostril discharge. Dogs can be protected by special vaccines administered either by injection or, in some cases, as nasal drops. Even if only going into kennels for a brief stay, dogs should always be vaccinated.

Tummy problems

There are numerous causes for tummy troubles in a dog but if you are worried or the symptoms persist for longer than twelve hours, you should consult your veterinary surgeon. If your dog has a minor tummy upset, you could try feeding him some rice or pasta cooked with chicken, or some other bland meal.

COMMON SYMPTOMS
- An affected dog may experience vomiting, diarrhoea, constipation
- There may be blood in the dog's droppings
- The dog may lose his appetite and refuse food
- Flatulence may be present
- The dog may eat or drink more than normal
- He may drink less than normal.

Vomiting

Vomiting may be simple and transient due to either a mild infection (gastritis) of the stomach or to food poisoning.

If severe, persistent or accompanied by other major signs, it can indicate serious conditions, such as distemper, infectious canine hepatitis, an intestinal obstruction, leptospirosis or a heavy worm infestation. In this case, seek veterinary attention urgently. The usual treatment for vomiting is to replace lost liquids (see diarrhoea below) and give the dog one to three teaspoons of Milk of Magnesia, depending on his size, once every three hours.

Diarrhoea

This may be nothing more than the result of a surfeit of liver or a mild bowel infection. However, diarrhoea can be more serious and profuse where important bacteria are present, in certain types of poisoning and in some allergies. Again, you should take your dog to the vet as soon as possible.

For mild cases of diarrhoea, cut out solid food, milk and fatty things. Give your dog fluids – best of all are glucose and water or some weak bouillon cube broth – little and often. Ice cubes can also be supplied for licking. Keep the animal warm and indoors.

Constipation

If your dog is constipated and is not passing any stools, it may be due to age, a faulty diet including too much chomped-up bone, or to an obstruction. Don't use castor oil on constipated dogs. Give liquid paraffin (a half to two tablespoons).

Where an animal is otherwise well but you know he is bunged up with something like bone which, after being crunched up, will set like cement in the bowels, you could get a suitable enema from the chemist.

Flatulence

'Windy' dogs may be the product of a faulty or changed diet. Often flatulence is associated with food that is too low in fibre although, paradoxically, too much fibre can have a similar effect. Generally, adjusting the diet to one of high digestibility and low residue will do the trick. Adding bran to the dog's food will alleviate many cases.

Blood in the stools

This condition can arise from a variety of minor and major causes. It may be from nothing more than a splinter of bone scraping the rectal lining, or the cause may be more serious, such as the dangerous leptospiral infection. Your vet will be able to identify the cause and advise on suitable treatment.

Malabsorption

Some dogs with chronic diarrhoea (often rather fatty looking), associated with a strong appetite but loss of weight, are not able to digest or absorb their food normally. The causes include enzyme deficiency (liver or pancreas faults) or disease of the bowel walls.

Your vet will employ a variety of tests to establish the cause and prescribe the appropriate therapy. Dogs that are deficient in pancreatic enzymes can be given pancreatic extract supplements with their food.

Polydipsia and polyphagia

Both of these conditions – polydipsia (drinking more than normal) and polyphagia (eating more than normal) – can be associated with diabetes, disease of the adrenal glands, kidney disease and other conditions. Careful examination of the patient by the vet, together with laboratory tests on blood and/or urine samples, is necessary to pinpoint the cause and thus lead to the correct treatment.

Salmonella infection

Salmonella is a type of bacterium that occurs in a wide variety of strains (serotypes) which may cause disease in, or be carried symptomlessly by, almost any species of animal. Sometimes salmonella can be found in the droppings of apparently normal healthy dogs. Dogs can contract salmonellosis by eating infected food, especially meat and eggs, or by coming into contact with rodents or their droppings, other infected dogs or, more rarely, reptiles or birds. The most common symptoms include diarrhoea (sometimes bloody), vomiting, stomach pain and even collapse, sometimes ending in death.

Diagnosis is confirmed by the vet sending away some samples for bacteriological culture and identification. The treatment is by means of specific antibiotics and fluid replacement. However, it is worth remembering that salmonella infection in animals may be transmissible to humans.

Parvovirus infection

This virus disease is spread via faeces. The incubation period is five to ten days and symptoms vary from sudden death in young pups, through severe vomiting, foul-smelling diarrhoea (often bloody), reduced appetite and depression to bouts of diarrhoea.

Treatment includes replacing lost fluid, anti-vomiting and anti-diarrhoea drugs and antibiotics. Puppies can be vaccinated against parvovirus from eight weeks of age either separately, or, best, in a combination vaccine against all the important canine diseases.

Acute abdomen

The sudden onset of severe pain, vomiting with or without diarrhoea and the collapse of the dog into shock is an emergency that necessitates immediate veterinary attention. The cause may be a powerful, rapidly-developing infection, obstruction of the intestine by a foreign body or a twist of the bowel itself, torsion (twisting) of the stomach, acute kidney, liver or uterine disease or poisoning. Successful treatment depends on quick diagnosis.

Urinary problems

Male dogs will urinate many times a day, in the course of a walk or a run in the garden. Bitches generally urinate less often. The usual signs of urinary disease are increased thirst and urination.

COMMON SYMPTOMS
- **Difficulty in passing urine**
- **Urination is frequent**
- **Blood is present in the dog's urine**
- **More thirsty than usual.**

Types of urinary disease

If something is wrong with your dog's waterworks, see the vet. Inflammation of

the bladder (cystitis), bladder stones and kidney disease are quite common and need immediate attention. Whatever you do, don't withhold drinking water.

Leptospirosis

This is the most common disease of a dog's kidneys. Humans can be infected by contact with dogs who suffer from this. Symptoms can be acute with loss of appetite, depression, back pain, vomiting, thirst, foul breath and mouth ulcers, or more chronic with loss of weight and frequent urination. It can be diagnosed by blood and urine tests and treated with antibiotics. Vaccination is also available.

Cystitis

This inflammation of the bladder generally responds well to effective treatment with antibiotics, such as ampicillin, perhaps together with medicines that alter the acidity of the urine and urinary sedatives.

Calculi

A diagnosis of stones (calculi) in the urinary system can be confirmed by your vet. In most cases, they are easily removed surgically under general anaesthetic.

Kidney disease

Kidney disease always needs careful management and supervision of an affected dog's diet. Chronic kidney disease patients can live to a ripe old age if the water, protein and mineral content of the diet are regulated, bacterial infection is controlled, protein is avoided. Prescription diets for chronic kidney cases are available from your veterinary surgeon and also from good pet shops. If you suspect kidney problems, see the vet immediately.

Skeletal problems

The most common skeletal problems in dogs are arthritis and slipped disc. Arthritis is much more common in elderly dogs than in young ones, and it invariably follows hip dysplasia.

> **COMMON SYMPTOMS**
> - **The dog may be lame**
> - **He may have difficulty getting up**
> - **His gait may be stiff, slow or unusual**
> - **There may be painful spots on bones or joints.**

Arthritis

This painful condition may arise from the congenital weakness of certain joints, their over-use/excessive wear, injuries, infections and nutritional faults. Treatment in dogs is similar to that used in treating humans, and your vet may well prescribe corticosteroids, non-steroidal anti-inflammatory drugs and various analgesics if your dog is affected. You may find that massages, perhaps with anti-inflammatory gels or creams, homoeopathic remedies and acupuncture can also afford relief and improved mobility in some cases. However, if you are considering trying out some form of alternative medical treatment, always consult your vet first.

You should avoid taking your dog out in very cold or wet weather, and buy him a snug, warm coat for outdoor use. Provide daily multivitamins and minerals and give elderly dogs, in particular, one to four capsules or teaspoons (depending on size) of halibut liver oil.

Painful joints

Arthritis can result in the thickening of the joint capsule, abnormal new bone forming round the joint edges, and wearing of the joint cartilage. The joint is enlarged and painful and its movement is restricted. It tends to affect the shoulders, hips, elbows and stifles in affected dogs.

Obesity

Carrying excess weight can put extra strain on a dog's joints. Slim down an overweight dog by modifying his diet (reducing carbohydrates and fats), feeding special canned slimming rations, desisting from giving him sweet titbits, and increasing his exercise gradually. Your vet may run a slimming programme: expert guidance will be provided and your dog's progress will be monitored by regular weighing.

Slipped disc

The dog's adjacent spinal vertebrae are separated by discs shaped rather like draughts pieces, which act as shock absorbers when functioning correctly. With the passing of time, as dogs grow older, the discs lose their elasticity and become more brittle, less compressible and degenerated. Then, a sudden movement or trauma can cause a disc to 'burst' with the discharge of crunchy material that piles up against the spinal cord or a nerve root with the consequent rapid onset of symptoms. The disc itself does not actually 'slip' out of line with the spine. Some breeds, particularly ones with relatively long backs for their size and short legs, such as Dachshunds, are more likely to suffer from this. It does occur, but less frequently, in Cavaliers.

Symptoms and treatment

The signs of a slipped disc include sudden onset of neck or back pain, paralysis or weakness of the limbs, loss of sensation, limb spasms and loss of control of the bladder. Accurate diagnosis is aided by X-rays. Treatment is by means of medication (analgesics, sedatives, anti-inflammatory drugs and anabolic hormones) and, in some instances, surgery to relieve the pressure on nervous tissues. Good nursing by the owner of the dog under veterinary advice is essential for the animal's recovery.

Skin problems

There are many kinds of skin disease that can affect dogs, and their diagnosis will always require examination and often sample analysis by the vet. If you suspect skin problems, do not delay and seek expert advice immediately before the condition gets worse.

COMMON SYMPTOMS
• **Thin or bald patches in the coat**
• **Scratching and licking**
• **Wet, dry or crusty sores.**

Healthy tips

• Feed a balanced diet with sufficient fats
• Never apply creams, powders or ointments without trimming back the hair. Let oxygen get to the inflamed area
• Groom your dog regularly to keep his skin and coat healthy.

Mange

This can be caused by an invisible mite and can be seen as crusty, hairless sores. Fleas, lice and ticks all cause damage to a dog's coat (see page 104). If you see or suspect the presence of any of these skin parasites, you must obtain a specially formulated antiparasitic product from the pet shop, chemist or your vet and treat your dog immediately. Powders are of little use against mange, and drugs in bath or aerosol form are more appropriate. Tough, deep forms of mange, such as demodectic mange, which is frequently complicated by the presence of secondary staphylococcal bacteria, may be treated by your vet using a combination of baths and drugs given by mouth.

As there are several different types of mange, you should ask the vet to advise you on the best method of treating your particular case. With all anti-parasite treatment of skin diseases, it is extremely important that you always carefully follow the instructions on the label of the preparation being used.

Ringworm

This subtle ailment may need diagnosis by ultra-violet light examination or fungus culture from a hair specimen.

Special drugs, which are given by mouth or applied to the skin, are used for ringworm. Care must be taken to see that human contacts do not pick up the disease from the affected dog.

Lumps and bumps

These may be abscesses, cysts or tumours and they may need surgical attention if they persist and grow larger. The earlier a growing lump is attended to, the simpler it is to eradicate, so you must consult your vet by the time it reaches cherry size.

Hot spots

Sudden, sore, wet 'hot spots' that develop in summer or autumn may be caused by an allergy to pollen and other substances. Clip the hair over and round the affected area with scissors to a level with the skin, and apply liquid paraffin. Consult your vet as the dog may need anti-histamine or corticosteroid creams, injections or tablets. Although they look dramatic, hot spots are quickly settled by treatment.

Nursing a sick dog

In all your dog's ailments, mild or serious, you will normally have to be prepared to do something to look after his welfare, usually acting in the capacity of nurse. This will involve learning some essential nursing techniques, such as how to take his temperature.

Be confident

When you are treating a sick dog, always adopt a confident and positive approach.

Be prepared and have everything ready in advance. Your dog will be reassured by your calmness.

Taking the temperature

You cannot rely on the state of a dog's nose as an effective indicator of his temperature, good health or sickness. As with children, being able to take your pet's temperature with a thermometer can help you to decide whether or not to call the vet and can also assist him in diagnosing and treating what is wrong.

You should use an ordinary glass thermometer, which you can purchase at most pharmacies. For preference, it should have a stubby rather than a slim bulb, or, better still, you can invest in an unbreakable thermometer, although these are more expensive. Lubricate the thermometer with a little olive oil or petroleum jelly and insert it about 2.5cm (1in) into the dog's rectum.

Once it is in place, you can hold the thermometer with the bulb angled against the rectal wall for good contact. After half a minute, remove and read the thermometer.

Temperature range

A dog's normal temperature will be in the range of 38–38.6°C (101–101.6°F). Taking into account a slight rise for nervousness or excitement, you can expect under such conditions to read up to 38.7°C (101.8°F) or even 38.8°C (102°F). Higher than that is abnormal.

Always shake down the mercury in the thermometer before use, and be sure to clean and disinfect the instrument properly afterwards.

Administering medicine

Try to avoid putting medicines into your dog's food or drink, as this can be a very imprecise method. However, for those dogs that are really averse to pills and capsules, you can conceal them in tasty titbits, but you must check that the dog has swallowed them.

Tablets, pills or capsules

These should always be dropped into the 'V'-shaped groove at the back of the dog's mouth while holding it open, with one thumb pressed firmly against the hard roof of the dog's mouth.

Liquids

These should be given slowly, a little at a time, by the same method or direct into the lip pouch with the mouth closed. They can be squirted through a syringe.

Handling your dog

It is very useful to know how to handle and restrain your dog effectively during visits to the vet, especially if he gets anxious about being examined or panics and may even behave aggressively and try to bite you or the vet.

Making a makeshift muzzle

A muzzle is essential when a nervous, possessive, aggressive or sensitive dog is in pain and has to be handled or

examined. To make one yourself, you can use a length of bandage, some string, a nylon stocking or even a tie – it will prevent you, the owner, as well as the vet being bitten.

By carefully positioning the muzzle not too far back on the dog, you can still administer liquid medicine by pouring it into the gap between the lips behind the encircling band. Here are the step-by-step instructions to making one.

Step-by-step instructions

1 Tie a knot in the bandage and wrap it around the dog's muzzle.
2 Cross the ends of the bandage at the bottom under the jaw.
3 Bring the ends round to the back of the dog's head and tie firmly.

At the vet's

It is important to know how to handle your dog when you visit the vet's surgery. Although some dogs trot in happily and do not mind being examined, others can be nervous and may even panic. Very large dogs are usually looked at on the floor, but the vet will want to examine small to medium-sized dogs on the examination table and you will have to lift your dog up if so.

Lifting your dog

To avoid injury, not only to your dog but also to your back, always bend your knees when picking him up. It is extremely important to support his body properly with one hand on his chest between the front legs and the other below his rear. This will help to make him feel more secure and reassured as well as preventing you dropping him. Even with a small dog, like a Cavalier, you need to bend your knees to avoid putting unnecessary strain on your back. Place one hand securely under your dog's rear and the other around his chest. Rise slowly up, keeping your back straight. Keep the dog in a secure position, holding him close to your body and bringing him up to chest height.

1 To lift your Cavalier King Charles Spaniel, gently bend your knees and then place one hand securely under his rear and the other around his chest. You can kneel down if wished.

2 With your hand at the rear taking most of the dog's weight and holding him securely, slowly straighten up, keeping your back straight. Support his chest with your other hand.

3 Keep the dog in a secure position, holding him close to your body, as you bring him up to chest height. You can then hold him with one hand, supporting his weight with your arm.

First aid

First aid is the emergency care given to a dog suffering injury or illness of sudden onset. The aims of first aid are to keep the dog alive, avoid unnecessary suffering and prevent further injury.

Rules of first aid

- Always keep calm: if you panic, you will be unable to help the dog.
- Contact a vet as soon as possible: advice given over the phone may be life-saving.
- Avoid any injury to yourself: a distressed or injured dog may bite, so use a muzzle if necessary.
- Control any haemorrhage: excessive blood loss can lead to severe shock and even death.
- Maintain an airway: failure to breathe or obtain adequate oxygen can lead to brain damage or loss of life.

Accidents and emergencies

In emergencies, your priorities are to keep your dog comfortable until he can be examined by a vet. However, in many cases, there is important action you can do immediately to help preserve your dog's health and life.

Burns

These can be caused by very hot liquids or by contact with an electrical current or various types of caustic, acid or irritant liquid. You must act quickly.

Electrical burns

Most electrical burns are the result of a dog chewing a live flex or cable, so wires should always be hidden, particularly from puppies, and electrical devices unplugged after use. Biting live wires can cause burns to the inside of the lips and the gums but may, in the worst cases, result in shock, collapse and death.

Recommended action First, switch off the electricity before you handle the patient. Examine the insides of the mouth and apply cold water to any burnt areas. If the gums are whiter than normal or blue-tinged, shock may be present. You must seek veterinary advice.

Chemical burns

Burns can also be caused by caustic chemicals, and you must seek veterinary attention if this happens.

Recommended action Wash the affected area with copious warm soapy water and then seek veterinary advice.

Scalding with a liquid

Hot water or oil spillage commonly occurs in the kitchen. Although the dog's coat affords him some insulating protection, the skin beneath may well be damaged with visible signs only emerging after several hours have passed in many cases.

Recommended action You must apply plenty of cold water immediately to the affected area and follow this by holding an ice pack on the burn – a bag of frozen peas is ideal. Then gently dry the burnt zone with mineral oil (liquid paraffin) and seek veterinary advice.

Poisoning

The house, the garden and the world outside contain a multitude of substances, both natural and artificial, that can poison a dog. If you suspect that your dog has been poisoned, you must contact your vet right away. Frequently some symptoms, such as vomiting, blood in the dog's stools or collapse, which owners may imagine to be the result of poisoning, are actually caused by other kinds of illness.

A dog may come into contact with poisonous chemicals through ingestion or by licking his coat when it is contaminated by a noxious substance. Canine inquisitiveness and the tendency to scavenge can lead dogs to eat or drink some strange materials. Sometimes owners will negligently give dangerous substances to their pets. Occasionally, poisonous gases or vapours are inhaled by animals. All our homes contain highly poisonous compounds. Poisoning can also be caused by certain plants, insect stings and the venom of snakes and toads.

Poisonous plants

Dangerous plants include the bulbs of many spring flowers, holly and mistletoe berries, the leaves and flowers of rhododendrons and hydrangeas, leaves of yew, box and laurels, sweetpea, wisteria and bluebell seeds, and all parts of the columbine, hemlock, lily of the valley and ivy. Some fungi are as poisonous to

---

COMMON POISONS
- **Mouse and rat killer**
- **Sleeping tablets**
- **Carbon monoxide gas in faulty heaters and car exhausts**
- **Weedkillers**
- **Corrosive chemicals, such as acids, alkalis, bleach, carbolic acid, phenols, creosote and petroleum products**
- **Antifreeze**
- **Lead paint, solders, putty and fishing weights**
- **Slug pellets**
- **Insecticides**
- **Rodenticides (warfarin)**
- **Herbicides**
- **Illegal bird baits.**

---

dogs as they are to humans, as are the blue-green algae that sometimes bloom on garden ponds in hot weather. Keep your dog away from these plants.

COMMON SYMPTOMS
The symptoms of poisoning vary but they may be evident as:
- **Digestive upsets, especially vomiting and diarrhoea.**
- **Difficulty in breathing.**
- **Convulsions.**
- **Uncoordinated movements or even coma.**
Note: If any of these occur in your dog and you suspect poisoning, you must ring the vet immediately.

Recommended action Determining which poison is involved can be quite difficult if you don't know what the dog has come into contact with. Professional diagnostic methods at the earliest opportunity are vital.

1 Look for any evidence of burning or

blistering in the dog's mouth caused by corrosive poisons.

2 Flush out the mouth with warm water and let him drink water or milk.

Corrosive substances

1 Wipe clean the contaminated area with rags or paper tissues and cut off congealed masses of hair with scissors. Cooking oil or petroleum jelly will help soften paint and tar.

2 Wash thoroughly with dog or baby shampoo and rinse well. Don't use paint thinners, concentrated washing detergents, solvents or turpentine.

Note: If the poison has been swallowed recently (within one hour), try to make the dog vomit by giving him either a chunk of washing soda (sodium carbonate) the size of a large pea or some English mustard powder (half a teaspoon in a quarter cup of water for a Cavalier).

Bee and wasp stings

Painful, but usually single and with no serious general effects, insect stings require little more than removal of the sting itself in the case of bee stings (wasps and hornets do not leave their stings behind) by means of tweezers and the application of antihistamine cream. Rarely, death can ensue if a dog is subject to a large number, perhaps hundreds, of stings. Stings can also be serious if the tongue or mouth are involved.

COMMON SYMPTOMS
- The dog's throat will swell.
- If he is allergic to the insect venom, he will go into severe shock.

Recommended action If your dog goes into shock, he will need anti-shock therapy, such as intravenous fluids, adrenalin and antihistamine injections. Keep him warm and make sure that his breathing is unimpeded while you obtain veterinary attention.

Snake bites

Britain's only venomous snake, the common adder, may sometimes bite a dog who disturbs it.

COMMON SYMPTOMS
- Two tiny slit-like punctures in the skin, which rapidly become surrounded by a zone of swollen reaction.
- Tremble, salivating, vomiting and staggering.
- The dog may then go into shock and collapse or even die.

Recommended action You must take the dog straight to the vet for treatment with adder anti-venom – do not delay.

Bleeding

The appearance of blood anywhere on a dog's body necessitates immediate close inspection. A variety of accidents and some diseases may produce blood from the nostrils, eyes or ears or in the droppings or in vomited material. None of the above types of haemorrhage are usually suitable for first aid by the owner. All need veterinary attention, however, though the causes may often be trivial and ephemeral.

Bleeding from the body surface through wounds inflicted during fights, traffic accidents or other traumatic incidents can be copious, and this does require prompt first aid.

Recommended action The most important thing you can do is to apply pressure to the wound. Hand or finger pressure is always invaluable until a pad of gauze or cotton wool can be found. This should be soaked in cold water, placed on the wound and kept in place by constant firm pressure or, better still, a bandage. Take the dog to a veterinary surgery as quickly as possible. Do not waste any time applying antiseptic ointments or powders to a significantly bleeding wound.

Heat stroke

Every summer we read in the newspapers of cases of dogs dying from heat stroke as a result of the gross thoughtlessness and negligence of their owners. Just like babies and young children, dogs who are left in hot, poorly ventilated spaces, particularly cars, and sometimes without water, will overheat.

COMMON SYMPTOMS
- **Inability to control internal body temperature.**
- **As the latter rises, the dog will become distressed, pant rapidly and will quickly weaken.**
- **The dog's mouth will appear much redder than normal.**
- **Collapse, coma and even death can follow in a reasonably short space of time, so you must act quickly.**

Recommended action Cooling the affected dog's body, particularly his head, by means of cold water baths, hosing and ice packs is essential. If the temperature-regulating mechanism in the brain has already been seriously damaged a fatal outcome may still ensue. Veterinary attention must be obtained immediately. Of course, by being a responsible and thoughtful owner, you can prevent such emergencies occurring.

Foreign bodies

These can occur in various parts of a dog's anatomy and treatment will vary according to the location.

In the eye

Foreign bodies in the eye will cause the dog to rub his head on the ground and paw at his eye.

Recommended action Flood the affected eye with human-type eye drops or olive oil to float out the foreign body. Do not use tweezers close to the eyeball.

In the ear

Plant seeds and grass awns are particularly likely to get into a dog's ears during summer walks. Their presence causes itching and irritation. The dog will shake his head and scratch and paw at his ears.

Recommended action Pour warm olive oil or other vegetable oil into the ear, filling it. The object may float to the surface and can be picked up by tweezers. Deeper, embedded foreign bodies will always require veterinary attention.

In the mouth

Pieces of bone or splinters of wood can become lodged in a dog's mouth. The offending object may be jammed between the left and right upper molars at the back of the mouth or between two adjacent teeth. Less commonly, an object, such as a small ball, gets stuck in a dog's throat. In all cases, he will show symptoms of distress, including pawing at the mouth, gagging, trying to retch or shaking his head.

Recommended action While someone holds the dog firmly, you should open his mouth and try to dislodge the foreign body with a spoon or kitchen tongs. Where the dog is having difficulty breathing and literally choking, try holding him upside down, massaging the throat and slapping his back. If you cannot remove the object, you must seek veterinary help at once.

In the paws
Splinters of glass, thorns, particles of metal and even fragments of stone can penetrate the pads on a dog's paws or lodge in the skin between the toes. As a result, the dog limps and usually licks the affected paw.

Recommended action If the object is visible, you can remove it with tweezers. If not, because of being embedded, then bathe the dog's foot two to three times daily in warm water and salt (a teaspoon of salt to a cupful of water) until the foreign body emerges from the softened skin. If lameness persists for more than a day or two, seek veterinary attention as infection may set in.

Fish hooks
You must never attempt to pull out a fish hook, wherever it is. Instead, use pliers to cut the end of the fish hook and then push the barbed end out through the skin. If it looks sore, rub in antiseptic cream. If you are nervous about attempting this, seek help from your veterinary surgeon.

Useful information

Organizations

Association of Pet Behaviour Counsellors
PO Box 46
Worcester WR8 9YS
tel: 01386 751151
www.apbc.org.ok

British Veterinary Association
7 Mansfield Street
London W1M 0AT
tel: 020 7636 6541
www.bva.co.uk

DEFRA
Ergon House, c/o Nobel House
17 Smith Square
London SW1P 3JR
tel: 020 7238 6951
www.defra.gov.uk

The Kennel Club
1–5 Clarges Street
Piccadilly
London W1Y 8AB
tel: 0870 606 6750
www.thekennelclub.org.uk

Magazines

Dog World
www.dogworld.co.uk

Dogs Monthly
www.dogsmonthly.co.uk

Dogs Today
www.dogstodaymagazine.co.uk

Our Dogs
www.ourdogs.co.uk

Your Dog
www.yourdog.co.uk

Websites

Animal Health Trust
www.aht.org.uk

Association of Pet Dog Trainers
www.apdt.co.uk

Cavalier Rescue
www.cavalierrescue.co.uk

The Cavalier King Charles Spaniel Club
www.thecavalierclub.co.uk

Honeybet Cavaliers
www.honeybet.co.uk

National Dog Tattoo Register
www.dog-register.co.uk

Pet Care Trust
www.petcare.org.uk

Pet Health Care
www.PEThealthcare.co.uk

Petlog
www.thekennelclub.org.uk/meet/petlog.html

Royal College of Veterinary Surgeons
www.rcvs.org.uk

Stavonga Cavaliers
www.stavongacavaliers.co.uk

Index